Octopus
Hunting

Richey Piiparinen

Illustrated by
Liz Maugans

**RED
GIANT
BOOKS**

This book is dedicated to
those sons and daughters of the Rust Belt.
To those we have lost to cancer.
To those who have cancer.
To those who have had cancer.
To those who have yet to have cancer.
This book is dedicated to those.

Table of Contents

Octopus Hunting

Relief Print "Toe to Toe"

Midnight
in
America

I am a researcher at Cleveland State University who focuses on the issues of city building, with an emphasis on how cities come to live, die, resurrect, or stay dead. The posterchild of that paradigm is a geographic area known as the "Rust Belt." The term's genesis came from presidential politics. In his campaign for a second term, President Ronald Reagan — through a paid hand, San Francisco ad man Hal Rinley[1] — ushered in the famous tagline "Morning in America."[2] It was a time when the Sun Belt was booming and California was dreaming. Conditions in the Industrial Midwest, though, were brooding. In a campaign stop at the LTV steel mill in Cleveland, Reagan's opponent, Walter Mondale, told the lunch-pail crowd that Reagan, through policies favorable to deindustrialization, was "turning our great industrial Midwest and the industrial base of this country into a "rust bowl."[3] The media reinterpreted Mondale's comments as "Rust Belt," a play off the terms "Sun Belt," "Cotton Belt," and "Bible Belt." Poof. The rest was history. Or currency. Depending on one's angle of view.

And while coined decades ago, it's a moniker still fresh in the nation's mind's eye, in fact making its presence in President Biden's 2022 State of the Union Address.[4] Referencing Intel's $100-billion-dollar decision to locate a semiconductor manufacturing plant in Ohio[5] —a signal, perhaps, that the rivers of disinvestment that coursed through these veins have in fact reversed course—a smiling Biden said, "If you travel 20 miles east of Columbus, Ohio you'll find a thousand empty acres of land and it won't look like much. But if you stop and look closely, you'll see a field of dreams...Let's bury the term 'Rust Belt." In the audience, the working-man's Senator from

Ohio, Democrat Sherrod Brown, a longtime admonisher of the term,[6] was beaming.

Map of the Rust Belt

Source Panther Media

With Biden still speaking, Senator Brown would tweet: "You're damn right we're burying the term 'Rust Belt.'"[7] If only it were that easy. As with most monikers that stick, the term is but a label of a reality, not just the reality of a label.

"What's in a nickname? Well, there's the definition of its component parts. Merriam Webster defines the word "rust" as "reddish brittle coating formed on iron especially when chemically attacked by moist air and composed essentially of hydrated ferric oxide."[8] Pretty innocuous, really. At least when it comes to "rust" as a noun. But the meaning of "rust" as a verb gets to the heart of the matter, giving credence to Senator Brown's concerns and to President Biden's proclamation "to bury" the term. That definition reads: "to degenerate especially from inaction, lack of use, or passage of time."[9] To degenerate. From inaction. Lack of use. Or passage of time. What does that sound like? It sounds like the process of aging and/or obsoleteness. It sounds like process of illness, dying, and death.

No wonder it's a detestable provocation. By contrast, the elicitation of "sun" in the regional nickname the "Sun Belt" lends itself to the notions of light, warmth, growth, and rebirth. Not to mention laughs, the beach, and good times. To cigarette boats and spirits donned with tiny, flamboyant paper umbrellas. Those are not the descriptives conjured up when thinking of places like Cleveland, Buffalo, Pittsburgh, or Detroit. When you think of those cities you're reminded that hard times exist. Or that life, while pregnant with possibility, is, well, pregnant with possibility. Things can go up, and things can go down. Things can go forward, and things can yank back. Things can breathe, and things can gasp. Steel can glisten, or steel can rust.

No doubt, the macroeconomic policies of deregulation, globalization, and decentralization—including, in the latter's case, the government subsidies that funneled jobs away from the union strongholds of the North into the right-to-work states down South—had a profound impact on what would become the proverbial postindustrial society. In 1969, for example, 43% of all private earnings in Cleveland's Cuyahoga County came from manufacturing. By 2021, the sector's share of earnings has contracted to 10%. Such is—as the German rock band, Scorpion, somberly put it— "the wind of change."[10]

Share of Private Earnings from Manufacturing in Cleveland, Cuyahoga County.

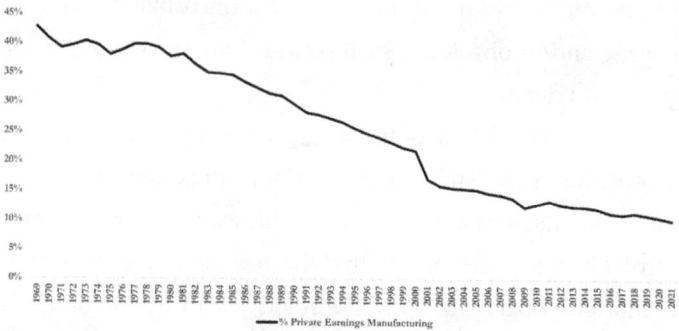

Source: BEA, 1969-2021, Table CAINC5S

"Globalization is by definition what characterizes the world today insofar as it is different from yesterday,"[11] explains the University of Pennsylvania's Center for Globalization Studies in an Urban World. That evolution can be succinctly described as a progression from an agricultural-, to industrial- to knowledge-intensive economy. Simply, the making of things has taken a back seat to the making of ideas, as that is where the value add is. After all, ideas fuel innovation, and innovation—through market-ready technologies—dictates what products are made, how they are made, and where and how they are delivered. These market forces, then, recontextualize our daily life, influencing what people buy, how people work, where people live, and how people interact. One only needs to look at the telecommunication company Zoom in the light of the global pandemic as exhibit A, B, and C, here, particularly as it relates to telecommuting and the subsequent effect on firm location, worker migration, and the capital flows that intertwine to form the two bookends of a city's being and becoming, namely, jobs and people. This is to say that innovation disrupts what was for what is and what will be, all the while tilting the gameboard of the market toward places willingly entangled in the macroeconomic present, like San Francisco, and away from places that've been chained to the macroeconomic past, like Cleveland. The issue for those in my field often boils down to the question: How does a region economically and societally evolve? How does Cleveland, for instance, break away from the path dependency that is the gravitational tilt of going down?

When it comes to the challenge of city building, think of a city as a feather in the breeze or a stick in a rapid of water. Global forces push and pull at places, ripping at a city's relevance. This relevance is often measured as indicators of civic pride. How many Fortune 500 companies does a city have? How many international flights? How many skyscrapers? Hey bucko, how big is your population? While these metrics are lauded by boosters and chambers of commerce alike, it is largely the stuff of locker room talk. More hubris than helpful. That's because beyond indicators of civic pride, a city's relevance can also be measured more tangibly: in the number of small businesses opened or closed, in the number of jobs gained or lost, in dollars on citizenry paystubs, and in hours on workers' punch clocks. And then, further downstream from these market forces, socioeconomic effects get played out. Think of socioeconomics—or the discipline that studies how economic activity shapes (and is shaped by) social processes—as where money meets mood. Because while the field is formally measured by drier, means-tested stats like median wage, poverty rate, and household income, those figures are but an abstraction to the blossom of ways money either gets you in on the American entrée or puts you out. And when on the outs, it's a process that can become encircling. Wrote author James Baldwin, famously: "Anyone who has ever struggled with poverty knows how extremely expensive it is to be poor."[12] The APR, for instance, on a pay day loan, notes the Consumer Financial Protection Bureau, is upwards of 400%.[13] Gulp. Socioeconomics is not only linked upstream to market factors, i.e., where's the jobs? what's the pay? but it also proceeds downstream toward human factors. Imagine our economic system as having an exerting, compounding effect on the quality of daily life, either crushing or enriching civil society. Is our economic system working in a way that provides fertile ground for care? Or are we scorpions in a bottle?

To the extent it does or doesn't, too, can be measured. This is illustrated in the murders and solved murders in the City of Cleveland since 1985. The city is moving in the wrong direction. On the downside, there's a city's incidences of trauma, addiction, hunger, infant mortality, assaults, murders, arrests, etc. On the plus side, there's the frequency of healthy births, good eating, pre-school enrollment, graduation, donation, public art, recreation, etc. Here, a city's success gets measured viscerally at the level of gristle and bone, with the quality of daily living ultimately manifest in the geography of the body. Not only in the spirit of the mind but also in the stuff of the flesh. This is where the rubber meets the road when it comes to a city's relevance in the global order of things. Or where the global order of things is patchworked and piecemealed by the living that live on the globe. After all, the individual mind and body is the wellspring from which all is collectively won or lost. It is the first and last home. The first and last stop on the track. It's where everything that's moving rests, and it's where everything that's dormant gets going. The key, here, is to realize that what settles at the bottom often flows from the top. This, then, is the importance of city building.

Homicides in the City of Cleveland

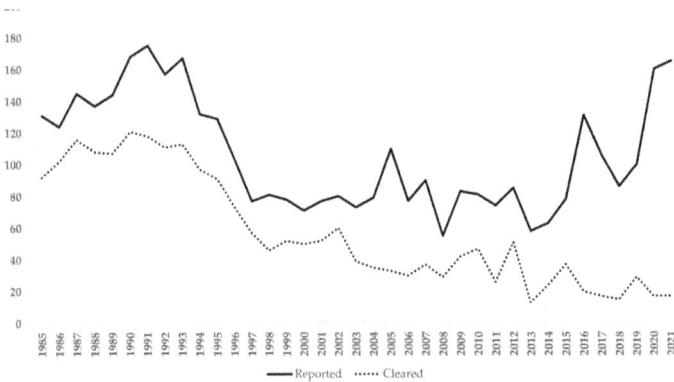

Source: FBI Crime Statistics, 1985-2021

That's my professional and collective experience. Now we cross into the personal and individual, landing into the geography of my body. While I study the life and death of Rust Belt cities, I also live it. I grew up in inner-city Cleveland, the Detroit Shoreway neighborhood on the city's West Side. I still live in inner-city Cleveland, the neighborhood of North Collinwood on the city's East Side. I am Rust Belt blue blood. Yet I never really saw Cleveland, or the Industrial Midwest, as relevant. I was born too late, 1976. I came out of the womb to see a broken place and will return there with not dissimilar visions at my back. And I will likely do so sooner rather than later. Despite my age, 46, the hands on my clock got rusted and ridged really quick. I learned in January 2021 that I got (so-far) incurable brain cancer, or glioblastoma multiforme: widely regarded as the most lethal of all cancers. Just Google it. But I've been handling the news somewhat gracefully. There was (and is) shock, yes. There was (and is) immense sadness, yes. But I wouldn't say hopelessness. Or helplessness. Rather, there's some vague seed of a sense of purpose that is skating the razor's edge of fighting for life while dying "right."

That brings us to these pages, which I began to compile—at first with clouded, anesthetized intent—right after diagnosis. They do not compile a memoir. Or a how to. Or a self-help. Rather, they string together as an act of creation, coming into form that is collected of essays. It is part cultural criticism, part city building, part psychology, part metaphysics, part pop culture, part art, and part illness. All written down in the context of home: The Rust Belt. It is a place I am from. It is a place that is from me. It is a place I bled in, and a place that bleeds from me. And while this mix of narrative nonfiction and subject matter expertise is not an existing genre per se—hard science, social science, humanities, metaphysics, and theology have long been dissuaded from cross pollinating, this reality an echo of the Cartesian mind-body dualism that dominates our discourse and, in turn, our approaches to constructing a shared, if shattered, reality—it's a genre-building that I have been doing for some time and even coined a name for it: "poetic policy." Consider the following an effort in the service of this new genre. Yet it's a genre in service of the need or a new approach. The way we are making cities in particular, and societies more generally, isn't working. As our domains of understanding splinter, so does the reality we are trying to understand. Whole societies can only be made so via a more holistic worldview. Explained T.S. Elliot in his poem, "The Rock", "Where is the wisdom we have lost in knowledge? Where is the knowledge we have lost in information?"[14] I gather it is in the reintegration of what's been pulled apart: land from body, body from mind, mind from soul, soul from spirit. It's a tearing collectively reflected in what sociologist Charles Cooley called "the looking glass self,"[15] in which the outside becomes the in and the inside the out. Or the self becomes the collective and the collective the self. And it's a reality ultimately made material in the bricks-and-mortar beehive that is the city, arguably that apex of the human settlement.

Granted, this collection of essays is a tricky project to pull off. There's America and its denial of suffering and death, if not an outright revulsion of it. We are drawn to happy things. Will anyone care? Then there's the practicalities. How long do I get? How long do I need? No matter. I've lost the luxury of hesitancy. Besides, there's things inside that need out, all of it actualized by the fact that my time horizon has come speeding into focus. And outside the window of my eyes a roadside sign blinks, asking perhaps the ultimate question for all of us. When does the will to hang on give way to the wisdom to let go? And what the hell do we fall into? Or, alternatively, what falls into us?

Will these questions find answers before the end gets done? Arguably not. Here, I bend to the founder of analytical psychology, the Swiss psychiatrist Carl Gustav Jung, who was equal parts empiricist, theorist, mystic, and practitioner. A true integrationist. Jung's corpus was defined by the questions that can be colloquially summarized as, "Who am I?", and "What's it all mean?" He treads there despite witnessing throughout the decades of his work that "the greatest and most important problems of life are all in a certain sense insoluble."[16] Yet while these questions can't be solved, observed Jung, they can be "outgrown," if only through the process of self-awareness.[17] "The meaning of my existence is that life has addressed a question to me," Jung wrote in *Memories, Dreams, and Reflections.* [18] Or, conversely, "I myself am a question which is addressed to the world, and I must communicate my answer, for otherwise, I am dependent upon the world's answer." Now, the world doesn't know the answer to my question. Nor should it. Nonetheless, the world breathes into the swelling of my urge for a full-throated response. And so here we are. Me. You. Us. Looking for hints at direction amid life's scavenger hunt for lost bodily function. Be it the body of a person, or the body of a place.

I think again of the term "Rust Belt." It's in many ways less a label of a region than a projection onto a region. It's America's answer to a regional reality America has cared less to know about. In that sense, one cannot bury what is continually dug up and never dealt with. The moniker the "Rust Belt" lives because degeneration, inaction, lack of use, and the passage of time lives. And because a collective denial of what's unfunny and unsunny lives. Yet while these facts of life can't be buried, they can be planted and outgrown. There is, after all, that which is giveth and that which is taketh away. Either way, you transcendentally adjust accordingly. Or you don't. Meaning, the only thing that is truly left behind into the dustbin of obsoleteness—whether it's a person, a neighborhood, a city, or a region— is that which fights, claws, groans, and wails to stay stuck, even as the windswept backdrop sashays forward, besides. Stuckness, even in its perpetuity, is a drag. There's nothing aspiring or enlivening about it. No matter what the phony angels of our better nature say.

As for the Rust Belt? Despite its warts, the people and place are tough stuff. Because while the region does exhibit a tendency to commune with the ghosts, there's an equivalent urge to slog forward through the ugly beauty of it all. There's no two ways about that. Or as the half[19] folkie, half rocker Neil Young put it, "Rust never sleeps.". Resilience—it's a hell of an attribute. Better than polish. Better than posh. Especially as the clock keeps ticking toward a period it would not be overstated to refer to as "midnight in America."[20]

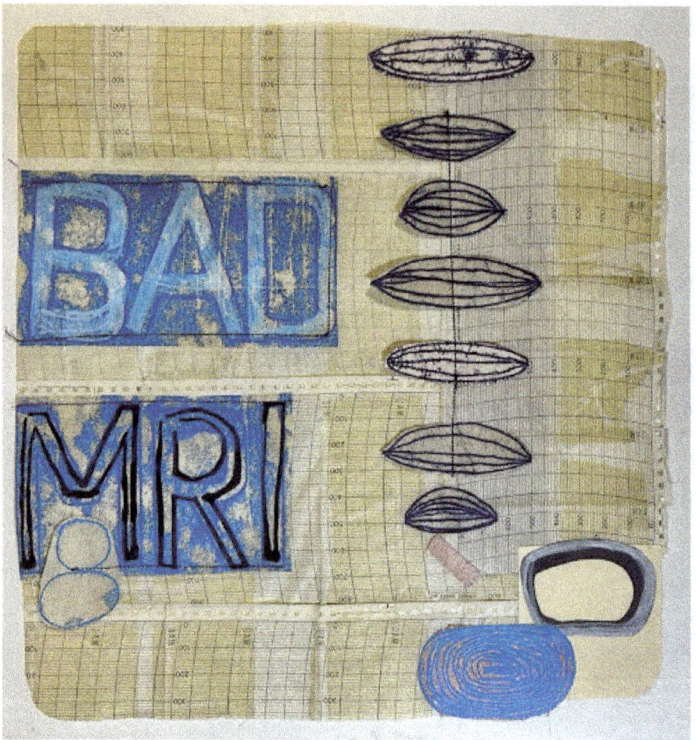

Mixed Media Print Collage on found scan paper, "Don't Wanna Know"

Standard of Care:

A Cover of Bon Jovi's Living on a Prayer

It started with a mutation that kicked off a cell division that birthed a brain mass that made me see things that were not there and to miss things that were. That's cancer purified. To take what was working and break it. To take what was pink and charcoal it. To take what was pliable and harden it. To take what was benign at worst, and beautiful at best, and change the parameters so invasive and scarred were the new bookends that bounded what's possible, if not probable.

It was Labor Day weekend 2020 when it formally made its announcement. I was lying in bed after a jog near the E. 72nd St. fishing wall, and a zig-zagging line, an aura, made its presence known in the upper-left field of my vision. It was small, multi-colored and shimmered. A one-sided headache followed. Classic migraine. I had them before, usually about once or twice a year. Then I got another aura later that day while watching the Cleveland baseball team. And then another the next day, and the next, etc. That was new. I immediately went to an eye doctor and neurologist. All clear, except for migraines and sinus headache. But then the auras kept happening, becoming more frequent. Eventually, my kids seemed to be blending into the couch and my wife blending into the bed. My eyes hurt looking at light. Evidence was amassing of abnormality. So, I went to a migraine specialist in December and again got the all clear. But she ordered an MRI just to be sure. I knew it was needed. I knew something be.

In the MRI machine I felt exposed like a sausage whose casing was opened. If a thing is flawed, an MRI has a good chance of finding it. Like standing naked in front of the bathroom mirror except inside out and times a million. The MRI made horrible sounds like bad laughing and "waw,

waw, waw, waw." Halfway through, the imaging tech said, "Uh, the doctor wants to add contrast." "Bad sign," I thought. Not just the unplanned introduction of contrast, but the fact my scan was being live-streamed to some doctor I never saw nor met. The MRI ended and the tech, a slightly older woman with classic, feathered Cleveland hair—a true *Drew Carey Show* extra—wouldn't look at me. I asked her if it was normal to have contrast added to a non-contrast order midway through. She mumbled, before saying, "I do what I am told." But then she slipped up and looked at me, and I saw in her eyes the memory of what she'd just seen. It was the last and first face I saw in my old and new life, respectively. I wonder if she wonders how I made out.

Minutes later I walked out of the changing locker and exited the sliding glass doors to enter the sunlit parking lot with its heated blacktop knowing that every hypochondriacal fear I ever had was coming out from under the bed and out of the closet to turn itself from a figment of my imagination into the flesh and bone of veracity. I drove home. An hour or two later I got the call. Primary brain tumor suspected. But it was benign, right? No. But it was small, right? No. But it was curable, right? Silence. I barely remembered what happened after that. There was some kind of howl, and I stumbled downstairs toward my wife before calling my mom. I then shriveled into an existence that crystallized the trivialities away and left no wiggle room to pretend there's nothing to see here and that everything is awesome. It is where you will find me today.

"Just don't Google it," the nurse said as she was taking my blood pressure. "It's all bad." "Smooth," I thought. She was speaking about my diagnosis, glioblastoma multiforme, and the prognosis you get when you Google it. But it was too late. I was by then six weeks out of my diagnosis and four weeks out of my craniotomy. It was thus Googled, it was lit reviewed, etc. I knew enough. I knew my type of cancer was blithely nicknamed the "terminator," as uncouthly laid out in an analysis out of the Proceedings of the National Academy of Sciences called, "Glioblastoma multiforme: The terminator."[21] So, I knew. I knew. I knew. I just didn't know how I felt.

Thankfully, brain cancer is rare, accounting for only 1% or so of cancers.[22] My cancer type, while making up 60% of malignant brain tumors, only gets diagnosed in roughly 20,000 Americans annually out of a population of about 329 million.[23] So it's kind of like hitting the lottery. The jackpot. Experts have no idea what causes it. It's not like smoking and lung cancer or sun exposure and skin cancer. The etiology of gliomas, including glioblastomas, are still seen as random mutational events. Hiccups in nature. Landing in the afflicted like bombs with fuses that never really end or start. Whether they are placed there by the hands of gods or devils, I am not sure. Regardless, relatively few are touched. Perhaps that explains why there has been so little headway treatment-wise, as the median overall survival of about 12 to 14 months has barely budged in decades.[24] Simply, there's no money to be made in a disease that not enough people get. There's no money to be made in a disease that people die from too quickly. A cash cow, then, this ain't. But what brain cancer lacks in commonness and chronicity it makes up for in cruelty and lethality. It's the leading cause of death from illness for those 40 and under,[25] and it's overtaken leukemia as the foremost cause of cancer deaths in children.[26] What a vile, pointless existence. What a black hole of possible time spent. Inertia attempts to ask the question, "Why me?" The question sits in my head like a rock. A big, unserviceable rock. But it's not hard to not dwell on it. Not only is it not answerable, it's myopic. "To the dumb question, 'why me?'" pondered writer Christopher Hitchens when given months to live with esophageal cancer. "The cosmos barely bothers to return the reply: 'why not?'"[27]

It was early Springtime in Cleveland, 2021. The weather patterns were jumping from lamb to lion to lamb to lion again. In between, colors were popping up and then kneeling back down by morning's frost. Each successive day is a display of the razor's edge that is the oscillating, slow-motion hand-off of winter's grip. A sunny, deep blue sky is met with a biting wind. The birds' songs give way to the noises of Lake Erie crashing violently. Everything is edging and a continuum. Yet it's hard to see. We are conditioned for Machiavellian endpoints. It's cold. Then it's hot. You're here. Then you're not. Never mind the multitudes in between. My life, too, is being lived on a line. Am I dying or living? Where am I going and where was I? What's up ahead and behind me? Meanwhile, each side of the line is a tilt toward the opposite of itself: Accepting loss and believing otherwise. Saying goodbye and saying hello. Fearing and finding the stillness in me that goes beyond fear, or me, for that matter. Losing that peace to be left with the fear in me and of me.

My home office is in a four-seasons room that sits beside a side porch that's edged by a small garden. Outside the windows, things are becoming less bare by the day. Lilacs, birds, grass, bush twigs with green buds. It makes me think about last Spring when COVID hit. Everyone's world went upside down just as the earth's colors were shooting out sideways. A landscape of party favors. Then all of a sudden, indiscriminate dying made its presence known in peacetime and late capitalism. It was a first for most of us. We were supposed to have evolved from this. But there we were, getting shut in and shut down. Lotioning our body with hand sanitizer. Hoarding toilet paper. Popping horse dewormer. Animals we were. To be honest, the reminiscing of last Spring made me sad, if selfishly so. I longed for those days when death's approach could be distanced through doable, reasonable precautions: washing hands, wearing a mask, separating my body from your body and my breath from your breath. Getting vaccinated. Now, death's approach is laser-pointed at me. I feel less together. Not to mention that there are far fewer pathways to remain not got. Perhaps it's a reflection of the fact that the crosshair on me is not coming from the outside in but from the inside out. The most prevalent path of escape is what's dubbed the "standard of care" in medical parlance.[28] For glioblastoma, like most cancers, this is the equivalent of cutting, burning, and poisoning, or surgery, radiation, and chemo. None of which are considered curative in my case. Instead, they are flesh offerings to gods to buy time. Which I'm down for.

Surgery happened and was as successful as possible, though the stay in the neuro ICU was a beast. I was in there for nearly 10 days due to issues related to releasing the intracranial pressure that slow-burned until it didn't, ultimately whizzing out of my increasingly gummy awareness like the whistle on a pressure cooker that petered out. My body hooked up like a game boy. Injections and pills around the clock. Not to mention I was there during the height of COVID's first big wave. The ICU was at capacity. The neuro ICU was taking on the backlog of the breathing ICU. Cleveland was coughing. Those late January nights there were long and cold and spiritless. It was hell in a hospital. Things were proceeding just fine a year ago. My mind, my body, my wife, my kids, my future...all intact. How did the world shatter so fast? Precipitated, so it was scribed, from a "pestilence that stalks in the darkness and a plague that destroys at midday." [29]

A week before I got out, an older Black woman was gurneyed into the room next to me, wheezing. I felt her aloneness through the partition. In her aloneness I felt my aloneness. We were alone together. But I also felt my fear. Hearing her cough, I envisioned the virus spreading like we were told it did. Mists. Puffs. Aerosols with spike proteins that bite you like a bat. I curled up on a hospital bed with my measly paper mask, thinking, "This can't be right. COVID patients next to cancer patients?" But I didn't have the energy to protest. I didn't have the will to disrespect. Anyway, there's dark, and then there's dark. That night the lightlessness seared. "Even though I walk through the valley of the shadow of death..."[30] But I escaped and made it out. She died, leaving Cleveland the next day. Hopefully headed to the light from whence she came.

A month after surgery, I began the poisoning and burning. I did a six-week cycle of combined radiation and chemotherapy. Each night I took an anti-nausea med followed by a chaser of Temador. Then each morning I laid on a radiation table, and my head was locked into a heat-fitted mask that's bolted in to ensure there's nowiggle room. Frequently, music played overhead. One time it was a cover—a cover! —of "Living on a Prayer"[31] by Bon Jovi. Another time it was the Bangles' "Eternal Flame."[32] "Is God fucking with me?" I thought. Or are we all just ants on a hill in which the logic and harmony of intelligent design inevitably gives way to the senseless surreal that's experienced all by yourself?

Photo, Getting radiation, all strapped in.

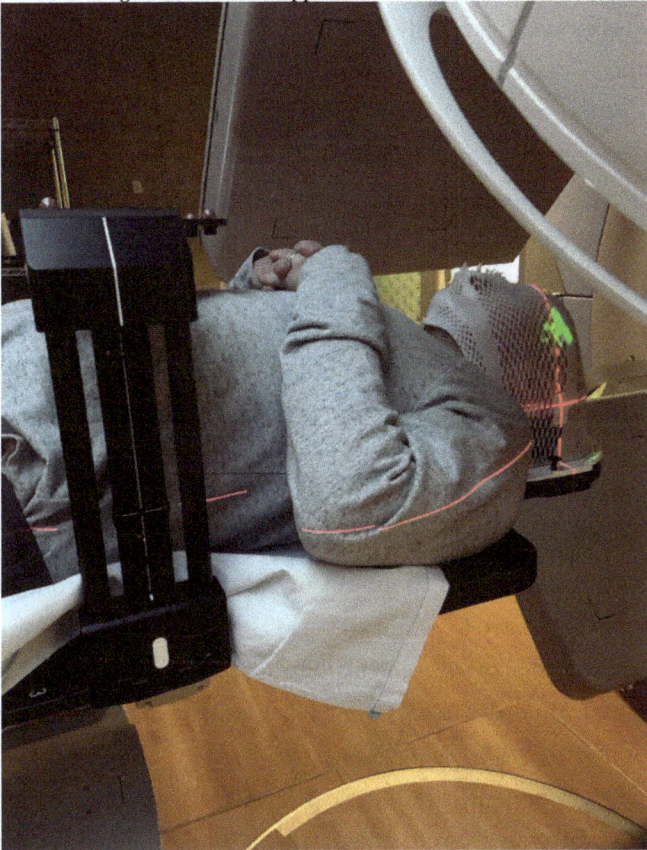

Source: Richey Piiparinen

But you got to believe, right? My doctors tell me this. My family and friends tell me this. And I tell it to myself. And I did. I believed through my behavior. I worked and work and work out daily. I took and take my cocktail of supplements, including Turmeric. Fish oil. PSK-16, Boswellia, Grape Seed Extract, the mushroom extract Turkey Tail, Berberine, B-12, and Green Tea extract. I tried to meditate, eventually learning a technique called the Microcosmic Orbit related to the practice of Qigong. I am current with the latest clinical trials that match my tumor biomarkers. I fight to join the ranks of the less than 20% of patients to survive to the two-year mark, or the 5% of to hit the five-year survival mark.[33]

Put another way, I live on the line. It's a tightrope walk between realism and optimism. You tip too far one way and you can get pessimistic really quick. You tip too far the other and you can fall into a state of suspended animation that is your head in the clouds. A few weeks into treatment I talked to my then-neuro-oncologist about this—a youngish, up-and -comer who came to Cleveland after having cut his teeth at Northwestern and University of California San Francisco— about how hard it was balancing in between the wish for life and an honest to Pete acceptance of death. A true, mucousy relenting. One not of the garden variety. I explained to him that in order for me to give it my all I had to confront the reality that I have to give it all back. He remarked that "few of his patients" take such an "insightful approach." "I got it," he went on. "In order to get to one place, you have to go through the other." "Yes," I said. "Yes."

As treatment continued, I eventually began finding that progressing from one headspace to the next means differentiating between the concepts of "belief" and "faith." "Belief," explained British philosopher Alan Watts, a former Episcopalian priest, "is the insistence that the truth is what one would wish it to be. The believer will open his mind to the truth on the condition that it fits in with his preconceived ideas and wishes."[34] "Faith," continues Watts, "is an unreserved opening of the mind to the truth, whatever it may turn out to be. Faith has no preconceptions; it is a plunge into the unknown."

Like most, I hate not knowing. But as I continued to standardize care, I began to hate the unknown less, if only because when you are made to live on the line you gotta accept you've got no choice. Not knowing is living. Besides, people believe themselves to death all the time.

Fatalism, or the subconscious belief in death's denial that gives rise to the unconscious want for death's approach, is a psychic phenomenon Sigmund Freud called "Thanatos," or the death instinct.[35] It's the compliment to Eros, or the "life instinct." One way to explain Thanatos is that by subconsciously forcing the hand of the unwanted yet inevitable we believe to control what we can't control. Not unrelated is Camus' concept of "liberation in suicide" that pockmarked much of the author's work. "Se suicider, c'est faire preuve de sa liberté," pondered the fictional character Mersault in Camus' classic *The Stranger*.[36] Today, Thanatos is a reality stranger than fiction. Over 1 million coronavirus deaths and counting in America,[37] more than double that of Americans killed in WWI and WWII combined.[38] So much of it was stoppable, yet so much of it was run into headlong. Of course, the irony is that the avoidance of pain only hastens its creation. In a story in the Jackson Free Press entitled, "'We Have Forgotten Who We Are': Denial and Death in Mississippi Hospitals,"[39] the journalist writes: "A patient in her unit refused to believe their diagnosis was real. 'They told me I tested positive, but I don't believe it,' the patient said. 'I'm ready to go home.'" But she never did.

I remember the day before I left the hospital after brain surgery, I noticed that there was a group of orderlies hanging outside the door of the patient next to me. They just stood. Not uncoolly. Then I heard shouting, "I don't believe you. I don't believe you. It is not even real." "What's going on?" I thought. "This is all getting next-level." I had a bevy of staples in the middle, back of my head. I later learned that the man yelled in response to the news that his wife just died from COVID. Day after day, more and more was making less and less sense. The whole hospital carried with it a smoggy air of exhaustion. Believers, deniers, whatever. You could feel the struggle of the collective to take it all in. Oxygen. The new normal. The creepiness of the humanly fallible. You name it. I, too, was ready to go home. Soon enough, I did. Forever indebted to those Clevelanders who cared for me. Forever recalling how dark and dispirited the halls of the hospital got. I never want to go back to that feeling again. It wasn't a sadness. Sadness is crystal clear. Rather, it was a sad-tinged madness. The worst of all worlds. Down, irate, and passionately unbeknownst.

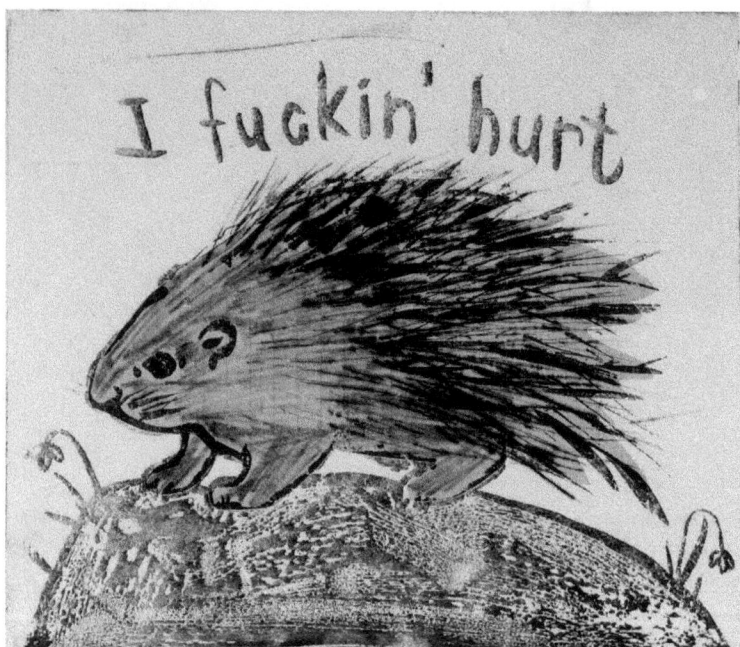

Etching, "Come Get Some"

The Cleveland Joke

I grew up on a Rust Belt street in a Rust Belt city: Colgate Avenue in Cleveland, Ohio. The street had an alley. It had working-class kids born to working-class parents. Life on the street wasn't idyllic. But that's not how life is, particularly in Cleveland. The city can be exceptional in its realism. "America has only three cities: New York, San Francisco, and New Orleans," said playwright Tennessee Williams. "Everywhere else is Cleveland."[40] Woof.

I remember my neighbor's house, olive green with aluminum siding. The Mills family lived there. Mr. Mills, a Kenny Rogers lookalike, came up from West Virginia along the Hillbilly Highway for a job, well, in the mills. But by the mid-1980s the family left, moving to the bungalowed-suburb of Middleburgh Heights. Their American Dream was Cleveland's American nightmare. By 1990, the city's population declined by nearly 40% from its peak.[41] The loss was due to folks like the Millses leaving, coupled with a growing absence of people moving in.

The lack of people arriving couldn't be blamed on an unaccustomedness with Cleveland. Throughout its history, the city never lacked for press, both the shaming kind and the lauding kind. But it was the shame that stuck. And it's the shame that persists.

Cleveland's shiniest badge of dishonor came from a 1969 piece in *Time* magazine called "America's Sewage System and the Price of Optimism."[42] "Almost every great city has a river," it began. "The poetic notion is that flowing water brings commerce, delights the eye, and cools the summer heat. But there is a more prosaic reason for the close affinity of cities and rivers. They serve as convenient, free sewers." The story would go on to highlight a small fire a few months prior on Cleveland's Cuyahoga River. "[The Cuyahoga] oozes rather than flows" the piece read. A photo was shown of firefighters using water to put out a fire on water. And while the picture *Time* used was not even from the fire in 1969 — the one shown was from a fire on the Cuyahoga back in 1952 — it was the optics that mattered, the visual conveying that Cleveland was a place that commits unholy acts. The sin was immortalized by Los Angeles-born singer Randy Newman in his 1972 classic "Burn On."[43] In it, he wrote:

> Now the Lord can make you tumble;
> And the Lord can make you turn;
> And the Lord can make you overflow;
> But the Lord can't make you burn.

Yet the assignment of shame onto Cleveland went beyond the fact water wasn't made to catch fire. Fires were common on the Cuyahoga throughout the early 20th century, like the 1952 fire pictorialized in the Time piece. But the previous fires failed to capture the public's imagination. That's because Cleveland circa 1952 was peak Cleveland—peak industry, peak population, and peak civic pride. Its public campaign was that of "the best location in the nation,"[44] and it was absorbed with plausibility. Then, Cleveland was simply known as a city that made things. That exported things. Where men worked, factories hummed, and where the bacon was brought. All this making made the region richer, with the relatively "benign" byproduct being the factory waste that was let outside to burn. The river fires during peak Cleveland were not unnatural as such, but rather the "price of optimism", as described in the *Time* piece.

Optimism was a legitimate outlook for the region before it wasn't. The area bounded by Detroit, Cleveland, and Pittsburgh was the nerve center for steel production and metal refinement, with Pittsburgh producing upwards of 60% of the nation's steel by 1910,[45] and Detroit making the bulk of the nation's cars[46]. Simply, the Industrial Midwest mattered, and this was never more the case than in the lead up to World War II.

On December 29th, 1940, President Roosevelt delivered a fireside chat on national defense called "The Great Arsenal of Democracy."[47] Roosevelt borrowed the term "arsenal of democracy" from General Motors' CEO Bill Knudsen, who had been called on by the President that May to discuss whether or not the nation's manufacturing sectors could be retooled to make, among other things, guns, planes, bullets, and tanks.[48]

"This is not a fireside chat on war," Roosevelt began. "It is a talk on national security; because the nub of the whole purpose of your President is to keep you now, and your children later, and your grandchildren much later, out of a last-ditch war for the preservation of American independence, and all of the things that American independence means to you and to me and to ours." Roosevelt would go on to explain that the "American industrial genius, unmatched throughout all the world in the solution of production problems" has been called into action, and that the cooperation between the government, industry, and labor was paramount in his belief that the Axis powers were "not going to win this war."[49]

The subsequent output from the "arsenal of democracy" was staggering. Detroit, while making up only 2% of the nation's population, produced 10% of the nation's war products.[50] Cleveland, too, was doing its part, producing a quarter of the nation's airplane parts.[51] Local firms pivoted in innovative ways: Sherwin-Williams went from paint to bombshells —Apex Electrical Manufacturing from vacuum cleaners to machine gun mounts — Bishop and Babcock Manufacturing Company from beer coolers to artillery shells — The Ferro-Corporation from porcelain to thermite.[52] Cleveland's collective effort was far-reaching, and the city was mindful of its impact. "Regardless of whether he's in a bed in the barracks," boasts a wartime columnist, "in a shelter tent or hammock; in a mess hall, hospital or sick bay; in a front-line machine-gun nest or fox-hole; cooped in a clattering tank or in a fighting aircraft or at a man-o-war battle station, it's a safe bet that there's a piece of Cleveland-produced business ready at hand or nearby."[53]

This reach would remain after the war, particularly during that period from 1945 to 1960 known as the "Golden Age of Capitalism."[54] With Europe in ruin, it was a period in which American hegemony was built, constructed off the backs of a growing middle class. Economists note it as a time of unparalleled productivity and consumerism. People who didn't have their own cars, homes, and washing machines before the war had them after. It was textbook consumer-side economics: Pay the unionized worker enough to buy what companies produce, the firms get the profits and hire more workers and make more customers. Notably, it was the geographies of goods production that won the day. Metropolitan Detroit had the nation's highest per capita income in 1960,[55] with Cleveland close behind.

But life comes at you fast. By 1969 Detroit had the 24th

largest per capita income in the nation, with Cleveland 25th. San Francisco was 3rd.[56] The regional fall would only continue. Peak Cleveland had peaked. "The city was worn out and feeble," observed a writer for the *Saturday Evening Post* in 1967.[57] "Its hands shook." The popular bumper sticker at the time read cryptically, "Pray for Cleveland."[58] This abrupt turn from civic pride to civic pain was palpable, an airiness perhaps best channeled by a young Cleveland poet named D.A. Levy, who "carried Cleveland around in his shirt pocket like some small clawed animal."[59] Levy's words stripped away any illusion of a Cleveland supremacy, with one verse reading: *Cleveland, I gave you the poems that no one ever wrote about you and you gave me NOTHING.*[60]

The price of optimism had given way to the cost of realism. 1952 Cleveland wasn't 1969 Cleveland. Water on fire wasn't requisitely magical but needlessly grotesque — the perceptual shift driven by a growing distrust of industrial landscapes, one encouraged by the decreasing economic benefits derived from such places. "Ironically, though the burning river would come to represent the costs of industrialization," explains the authors of "Perceptions of the Burning River: Deindustrialization and Cleveland's Cuyahoga River," "the growing reaction to the fire actually represented the process of deindustrialization."[61]

Deindustrialization — or the social and economic change caused by the reduction of industrial activity — is at its core a process of loss. These losses are touchable. The city shed 125,000 people during the 60s, followed by another 177,000 plus during the 70s. In fact, Cleveland's rate of loss in the 70s — an attrition of nearly 1 out every 4 residents — was second worst out of America's big cities, trailing only St. Louis.[62]

Population in City of Cleveland 1820 to 2020

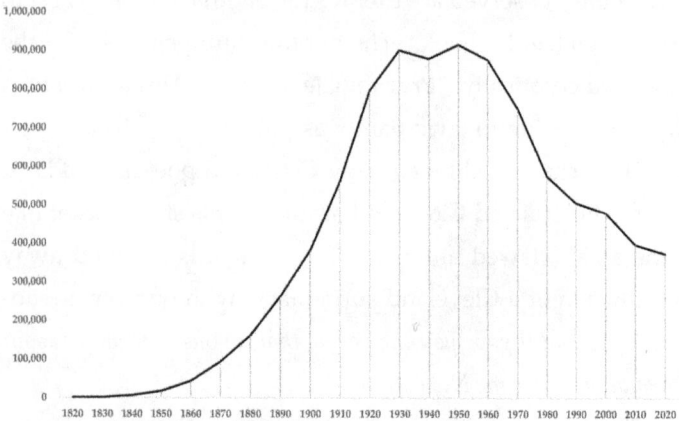

Source: Decennial Census, 1820 to 2020

The loss of people began bubbling up into the social and built landscapes. The city's housing stock started falling apart. Between 1969 and 1972, nearly 3,500 houses were abandoned in the city.[63] Arsons were rampant too. According to Daniel Kerr's analysis "Who burned Cleveland, Ohio? The forgotten fires of the 1970s," there were about 1,500 set fires in 1974, another 2,000 in 1975, before peaking to nearly 4,500 by 1979.[64] And cars were exploding. In 1976, there were 21 car bombs in Cleveland and another 16 in its suburbs, making Cleveland the "car bomb capital" of America, according to statistics compiled by Alcohol, Tobacco and Firearms Unit.[65] The bombs were employed for various reasons, explained *Cleveland Magazine* writer Edward Whelan in a 1977 piece entitled "The Bombing Business." But one reason stuck out. With the city's residents "inured to street violence, bombings, with their God-awful terror and indiscriminate destruction, retain their power to startle and shock — the last frontier of violence."[66]

One can envision, then, the feel of the city compounding: the fear and sadness of deindustrialization growing into
the fear and anger of violence that's cultured when big things
present themselves upon little people. Adding insult to injury was the fact that Cleveland became the first major city
in America to default on its loans in December of 1978.[67] And
so it all adds up to a fast fall from grace. Cleveland became
known as the "mistake on the lake."[68] A failure in the eyes of
the motherland that is your host nation. Cleveland became a
punchline. Of geopolitical proportions. On June 19th, 1981,

Ronald Reagan laughing at the Cleveland Joke.

Source: UPI

during a televised black-tie gala for President Reagan, co-median Rich Little stood before the President discussing the specter that was the Soviet Union. "'Mr. President, how do you plan to keep Russia from invading Poland?" Little then put the punch in the line, "I would rename it Cleveland."[69]

Reagan doubled over in his tuxedo. The room roared. Eventually, the Cleveland joke became an export. "In every country, they make fun of a city," quipped the Russian-born comedian Yakov Smirnoff. "In U.S. you make fun of Cleveland. In Russia, we make fun of Cleveland."[70]

Today, the Cleveland joke is old hat. It's in a long line of American traditions, like Thanksgiving, blue jeans, and bingo. Even now, a "TRAVEL.COM®" article from 2022 referred to Cleveland as "the Charlie Brown of cities."[71] Pshaw. Yet that the Cleveland joke still reverberates is less illustrative than why it was born in the first place. America subconsciously charged some meaning into the city and the region. It can be argued that the meaning was less about Cleveland and the Rust Belt taking it and more about America needing to give it—a defense mechanism known as "displacement" in the psychodynamic space.[72] Shorter, the nation is prolific in its collective capacity to disentomb what is commonly understood as blaming the victim. The inability to properly aid the commonwealth of Puerto Rico after Hurricane Maria rings in my ears. Of course, New Orleans and Katrina is legendary in this miserable regard.[73]

This does not, however, mean that the Rust Belt doesn't need to unwrap itself from the warm blanket of victimhood. The region most certainly does. As detailed in the *Cleveland Magazine* essay "The Man Who Made Cleveland a Joke," the

Cleveland joke was, after all, birthed by a Clevelander: *Laugh-in's* Jack Hanrahan.[74] But while making his bones out in Hollywood and writing jokes about his hometown Cleveland, Hanrahan is testament to the fact that home has a way when life hits the skids of pulling you back. In a 2007 *Cleveland Plain Dealer* article by Christine Jindra,[75] "From a comic career to a tragic life Emmy-winning writer now homeless in his native Cleveland," Jindra explains. Hanrahan—the second-youngest of 11 children who was raised Irish Catholic on the West Side of Cleveland— "spent his [twilight years] back in Cleveland wandering Cleveland streets and [going]...to St. John Cathedral every day for Mass, which he referred to as 'the magic show.'" "'I know this is a tragic story,'" Hanrahan would tell Jindra. "But it's got a happy ending. [He was crying I'm gonna live. I've got work to do." He'd die a year later at the age of 75 in a nursing home,[76] penniless and all by himself. Outside of the pink-collared Clevelanders who cared for him on his exit stage left. Shakespeare's tragicomedy has got nothing on Cleveland and its inhabitants. The only question that remains is whether what sits at the end of the heroic arc of the rainbow is a figure that's more Ulysses or Ahab. "I know not all that may be coming," writes Melville in *Moby Dick*, "but be it what it will, I'll go to it laughing."[77]

Letterpress relief from vintage dingbats, "Chip Off the Old Block"

Descent
with
Modification

Every story is bounded within a bigger story, like a set of Russian nesting dolls. A person's pain or pride, for instance, is tied to a city's stories, which are tied to national stories, which are tied to world affairs. Cleveland's story is not just Cleveland's story. It's the story of a city in a region in a country in a world that's constantly changing. The key is to find patterns within this change. If only to know what's in your power as a person and what's in your power as a collection of people — a city — so the change is less random and disruptive and thus planned for.

Otherwise life is just one big shit show of pure emotion that's expressed by the powerful and dispensed as policy. And usually bad policy at that. Not just ineffective, mind you, but counterproductive: that creation of the thing you obstinately espouse to despise. This process of subconscious self-destructiveness—while less examined in the public policy space—is well-recognized in the field of analytical, or depth, psychology, where it's been dubbed by Carl Gustav Jung as the "shadow self."[78] When the crowd, for instance, chants "build the wall," is it a legitimate offer to amend immigration policy? Nah. It's a burp from the shared shadow self.

What were the larger stories that shaped the Rust Belt? Note the population trajectories of Cleveland, Detroit, and Pittsburgh from their inception until now. Each of their populations peaked in 1950. Then, Detroit was the 5th largest city in America, Cleveland the 7th, and Pittsburgh the 12th.[79] The heartland was a powerhouse of people. That each city reached peak population in that year, 1950, is no coincidence, as it represents a demarcation between one economic era, or that of brawn, and another, or that of brain.[80] That is, as the leading edge of the global economy evolved from agricultural- to labor- to knowledge-intensive, so shifted the migration patterns that flowed across the American topography, eventually pooling in places tethered to the new economic order and receding in places manacled to the past. And depending on what side of the line your city's economy was on, what sprouted was either growth or decline. Or jobs arriving vs. jobs leaving. Or prosperity accruing vs. poverty concentrating. To this day, the cities of Cleveland and Detroit have the top two highest big-city poverty rates in the nation.[81] The effects of macroeconomic change, then, persist. As do cities' efforts to not get left behind.

Total Population in Deindustrialized Cities.

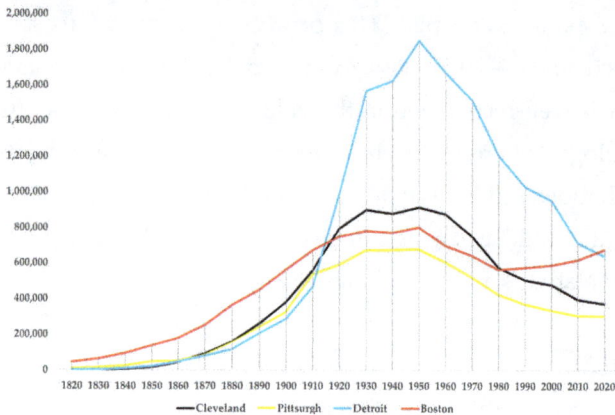

Source: Decennial Census

An exemplar, here, is Boston, which is no stranger to deindustrialization. In his paper "Reinventing Boston 1640-2003," Harvard economist Ed Glaeser tells of the city's "remarkable rebirth" from a "a dying factory town to a thriving information city," a conversion evidenced in its population trajectory.[82] Like the Rust Belt cities, Boston's population, too, peaked in 1950. Unlike the Rust Belt cities, Boston's population decline reversed in 1980, a reflection of its economic reinvention decades prior that put the region back in the path of migratory flows.

When we talk about an evolving global economy what are we talking about, really? This question, while wonkish and seemingly airy and impersonal, is important if you're trying to figure out why your city is the way it is, and why your prospects are the way they are. That's because what's global becomes local, like a butterfly flapping its wings in Brazil becomes a tidal wave that laps your back porch. This idea, then, of something coming from somewhere for some reason, and then coming at you before falling down into you and then out of you into the thing next to you—a chain of events in a complex system where all is webbed together—is useful in understanding how one's story is nested in relation to where their city fits in the grand scheme of things. Simply, knowing the context of your condition is just as important as knowing the state of your condition. Understanding the context surrounding the Rust Belt requires getting a grip on the macroeconomic backdrop. This can be partly realized through the use of two celebrated economic concepts. One is "economic epochs," and the other is "creative destruction." The former relates to what the global economy evolved from and what it evolved into. The latter refers to the process, or impetus, of change. What's the driving force of what Darwin called "descent with modification?"[83] In biology this is called "survival of the fittest." In evolutionary economics it's creative destruction.[84]

Economic epochs are characterized as distinct periods of economic history that are sparked by epochal innovations, described as "major breakthroughs in the advance of human knowledge, that constituted dominant sources of sustained growth over long periods and spread to a substantial part of the world..." so explains economist Simon Kuznets.[85] Crucially, the beginnings of an epoch make it so that economic activity clusters in areas of the world that hold comparative advantage. Rust Belt cities, for instance, had geographic advantages that paired well with the epoch known as the industrial revolution, which was essentially a time of entry for new manufacturing processes.

Pittsburgh, or the "Steel City," became so due to the region's "bounty of bituminous coal [that] was uniquely able to be used in the blast furnaces that transformed iron ore into pig iron," explains Pittsburgh economist Chris Briem.[86] A decades-old University of Pittsburgh study elucidated that coal and metallurgy came together in Pittsburgh "like twin supernovae, impelling into rapid expansion all elements of the economy which were aligned with them..."[87] Moreover, Pittsburgh's output, steel, became other regions' input, allowing Detroit, for instance, to be the "Motor City" via agglomeration of auto manufacturing plants and its requisite supply chains, with Cleveland a crossbreed between each: It had both steel mills and car plants.

In fact, if one looks closely at the topography of Cleveland one could see how the Cuyahoga River not only splits the city between its East and West Side communities but its industrial attachment to mining and metallurgy heading East and automobile manufacturing heading West. Moving eastward from the mouth of the Cuyahoga leads you from the still-existing Arcelor Mittal steel plant and pedestrian inclines of the Nerve Center for Steel and Cars.

The Rust Belt of North America

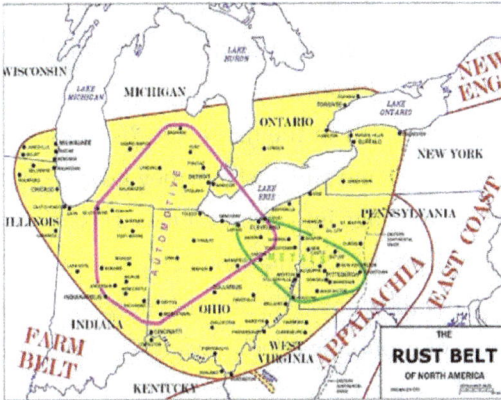

Source: https://www.coalcampusa.com/rustbelt/rustbelt.htm

Tremont neighborhood—complete with its Russian Orthodox spires made famous in the Deer Hunter's[88] wedding scene that'd give the movie its old ethnic, Rust Belt cred—before blending into the tilt down through Youngstown's Mahoning Valley and finally into the "Paris of Appalachia," Pittsburgh. That city of rivers, inclines, and even its own dialect: Pittsburghese, "Yinz are a buncha jag-offs," as the Pittsburgh folks say. Whereas the Clevelander would just put it thusly: "You guys are assholes." With a proper Midland accent accentuating and elongating the nasally "a" in the word "assholes."[89]

Westward from the Cuyahoga you move through the decidedly more gridded, Fordist landscape with streets

named "Chevrolet Blvd" that housed the old Chevy plant
and the still-standing Ford plant, proceeding toward the
curvatures around the Great Lakes past "the Islands" and
Klinger's Toledo with its Tony Packo's hot dogs until you
roll into the flat unravel that welcomes the onlooker into the
wide-open Grizzly Bear that is Detroit: a city whose 143
square miles is large enough to fit Manhattan, Boston and
San Francisco withinits borders.[90]

But as is embodied in the name epochs, these economic
time periods don't stand still. Instead, they flow, like a stream.
And as they do they age into change. Or as the Greek philosopher Heraclitus put it, "No man ever steps in the same river
twice, for it's not the same river and he's not the same man."[91]
In the context of economic epochs, what was unique and ad-
vantageous at the start of one economic era becomes ubiqui-
tous and ungainly as it grows old. In the case of the industrial
epoch, that meant investment, trade secrets, firms, supply
chains, and employment dispersing from the manufacturing
Heartland for locales that were more cost effective, be it off-
shore or down South. Who cares if Pittsburgh had the ingredients for steel? The recipe kept being improved upon so that
lots of other locales did too. Who cares if Detroit birthed the
assembly line? Other countries eventually did it better. Headlines a 1990 *Los Angeles Times* piece, "Assembly Line Flexibility Sets Japanese Apart."[92]

Meanwhile, as the Rust Belt was fighting and still fights to
squeeze blood from the stone that is its industrial heyday, another epoch—the information age—was being birthed, kicked
off in no small part by the epochal innovation that was the
microchip. Little of this digital innovation was being carried-

out in the Rust Belt but rather in the likes Northern California, Texas, and Boston. And as the age of information kicked off, the center of gravity shifted from the Rust Belt to places that had a toehold in the emergent order. This shift is evident when looking at the per capita income trends of select metropolitan eras from 1969 until 2021. The Rust Belt regions hold flat while San Jose, CA and San Francisco take off, with Boston diverging as well.

Per Capita Income Divergences. 1969 to 2021.

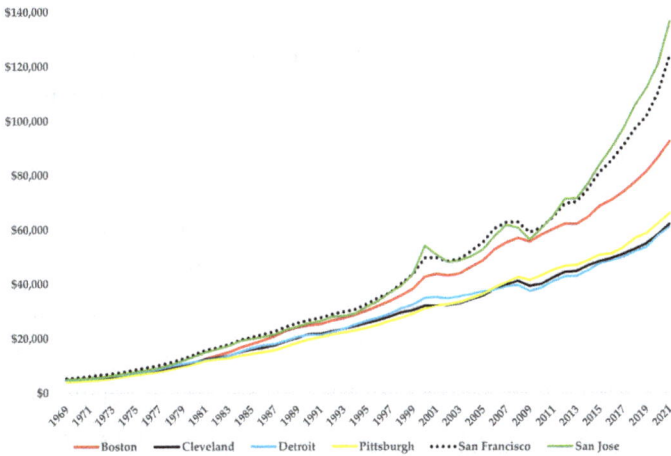

Source: BEA, Table CAINCI.

But technological advance doesn't just happen. The economy doesn't just evolve on its own like a gravity clock ticks. There's a rhyme and reason as to why technologies enter onto the scene where they do and when they do. And once the innovators' opportunities are had via the absorption of the arbitrage in the market, the effect is what economist Joseph Schumpeter called "creative destruction,"[93] which is simply the

process wherein new technologies make the older way of doing things obsolete. There was the horse and buggy, for example, and then there were cars. Now there is Zoom. The shep-
herds of creative destruction are scientists, researchers,
inventors and entrepreneurs who — while motivated by profit
— are also frequently driven by the collective good. After all,
the lifeblood of innovation is to find a better way. Or to make
what was harder easier, or what was scarce more abundant.

The agricultural epoch birthed a bloom in crop production, evolving the concept of horsepower so that it can substi-
tute for, well, horse power. The industrial epoch made the
limits of manpower more limitless by replicating it with com-
bustion, pistons, and gears. The information epoch created a
surplus of memory, unleashing information into our laptops
and handheld devices that don't forget with time.

Yet progress doesn't stop. Today, innovation is less
about access to information than it is making sense of it. It's
about knowledge. In fact, we have so much information that
we are drowning in it, leaving us less informed, or worse:
misinformed; or worse yet: disinformed, the latter defined
by *Oxford Languages* as false information "intended to
mislead."[94] The crux of the matter is that while information
is abundant, our ability to comb through it isn't. The human
attention span is limited. Explained Microsoft CEO Satya
Nadella, "Data is plentiful. Attention is scarce, and we'll
never get more of it."[95] Echoes author Eric Weiner, "we are
not information processing machines any more than we are
hunter gatherer machines."[96]

Enter Artificial Intelligence (AI). The AI epoch is making
the scarcity of human attention less so via the advance of cogni-

tive computing. It's the next epochal innovation to change the course of events, unleashing a boom in our ability to find a signal in the noise. As epochal revolutions go, it is just getting started. "[While we've seen the A.I. sun, we have yet to see it truly shine," writes Craig S. Smith in the *New York Times*.[97] "Researchers liken the current state of the technology to cellphones of the 1990s: useful, but crude and cumbersome.

As the AI epoch inevitably unfolds, it will—as epochs did before it—have a rippling effect across industries, firms, and products, not to mention the cities that make up the economic geography of those market entities. The Clevelands were kings during the industrial era. But then the Rust Belt lost its global relevance at the dawn of the digital age, and it's still fighting to claw it back. That's because economic evolution is not played out evenly across space. As creative destruction happens, some cities win, most lose. Some workers win, more lose. Some neighborhoods flourish, more need nourished. To the extent the Rust Belt can get back on the right side of history is related to whether or not it can unchain itself from its past.

Loss sucks, and being unmounted from the mantels of prestige, bounty, and security has a scarring effect. The Rust Belt is scarred. These scars run across its veins and course through the veins of its people. The marks are not only physical and geographic—abandoned factories, vacant houses, skeleton coal mines, black lung, cancer, flammable rivers, and brownfields filled with the sunset flowers of pollution—they are also perceptual and psychogeographic; that is, they exist as stimuli that forever serves to point the populace toward the night side of life. Consider the aesthetic a ubiquity of antiquity. In his book *The Aesthetic of Ruins*, for example, philosopher Robert Ginsberg comments that "ruin guides meditations upon our mortality and endangered world."[98] Put another way, the aesthetic reminds one to not get too high up on your horse else risk taking an arrow, and that the sound in the distance is most likely not a harp. But rather the sound of forced entry.

What has arisen from this interplay between place and person, or more accurately: between person, perception, and place, is a grounding malaise that is Midwestern modesty at its best and flyover country self-banishment at its worst. No one will mistake this region for being too aspirational. Or too carefree, Pollyannaish, and light. There's less heads in the clouds around here than clouds and bowed heads. "Decline is a fact of life," notes Congressman Dan Kildee of Michigan as he championed the demolition-at-scale policy in Detroit. [99] "Resisting it is like resisting gravity." That's a remarkable admission for a politician in the ten-gallon-hat culture of American politics and policy. And it's an admission that can only be coughed up from a politician that has canvassed in the likes of Flint and River Rouge. No matter, kudos to Kildee for touching the devil, flinching, and having the guts to talk about it. An issue, though, arises in that here's a fine line between realism and fatalism.[100] There's a fine line between holding on to what you got and turning the page to begin a new story. There's a fine line between pining for a manufacturing renaissance and being left in the dust of evolution again. In his report "Regenerating America's Legacy Cities,"[101] researcher Alan Mallach laments the Rust Belt's tendency to be "path dependent", or looking to what has happened in the past to make current and future decisions. For Mallach, history affects the present to the extent that it limits leaders' ability to see possibility. "Those who have never experienced anything but decline may have difficulty even conceptualizing a different reality," Mallach writes.[102]

Now, it is true that seeing is believing. This is the motto of our materialist, or physicalist, existence ever since— as Nietzsche famously wrote in *The Gay Science* at the dawn of the scientific revolution— "God is dead...And we have killed him."[103] But what's less recognized is that believing is seeing. Percept has the power to be real. Mind is more than just matter. The Rust Belt has been operating from a scarcity mindset, described as "when you are so obsessed with a lack of something...that you can't seem to focus on anything else, no matter how hard you try."[104] A scarcity mindset involves living with the ghosts in the landscape of nostalgia, archetypally embodied by the prom queen and high school quarterback that age in their lonesomeness with their too-tight costumes on. I think of the high school football foundry town in Pennsylvania that served as the backdrop in the 1980's movie *All the Right Moves* and how bitter and full of false promises it was. "You're not God, Nickerson," said Tom Cruise's character, Stefen Djordjevic, to his soon-to-be-ex football coach. "You're just a typing teacher."[105]

Such a milieu is exhausting for the next generation of pall bearers who didn't grow up in the cultural soup of their parents and grandparents. Those Boomers that crowd out what's unfamiliar, all the while refusing to not boom. Perhaps, then, everything the Rust Belt needed to progress from its economic past to its economic future is here and has always been here. To see that—or rather, to believe that—requires a collective readjustment of the horizonal sightline so it's beyond the purview of just gazing at the navel.

In the November 2021 *New York Times* article entitled "Jay Last, One of the Rebels Who Founded Silicon Valley, Dies at 92,"[106] the article discusses the life of Pittsburgh-born, Intel co-founder and star physicist, Jay Last. Last was a Rust Belt-bred seed of the information epoch. But he sprouted elsewhere. "When Dr. Last was finishing his Ph.D. in 1956," the article explains, "he was asked to take over as head of the glass lab back in Butler, Pa. where he worked during the summers. 'I went and told my parents'," he explained. "My mother said, 'Jay, you can do a lot better than that with your life.'" He did and took his creativity elsewhere, leaving his homeland to deal with the bits of its destruction. And thus, continued the Rust Belt's devolution. Or its descent without modification.

Mixed Media Print Collage, "As the World Drips"

Trickle-Down
Narrative
Economics

The younger Black nurse draws my blood, like she has done every Tuesday for the past five weeks. They are making sure my platelets don't crash from chemo. She looks at me. I'm looking down. I've been having a hard time looking people in the eyes since my diagnosis. Call it shame. Call it guilt. Call it shock from a sickness that hits more like a car accident than a time-lapsing condition. She wants me to look up. I can feel it. "Oh, we aren't friends anymore?" she asks. I nod. But I don't look up. She relents and pulls the needle out, then tapes the cotton ball I am holding to stall the blood. "Alright, you're set. See you next week." I nod again. She then prepares to drain another. We are an assembly line of broken figures. Part of what's called the "knowledge economy."

I leave the nurse's station and enter the waiting room of the outpatient lab at the Seidman Cancer Center in the City of Cleveland. People are all around. Mostly older. Many Black. Many White. Vastly working class. Universally struggling. Unanimously with cancer cells living in the brooks of their body, carried in there through the consequence of living in a world that is constantly falling on you and in you. Not unlike a game of Plinko in the *Price is Right*, but with the pegs bent severely toward the opposite side of winning—the deck stacked even worse than in the gameshow.

In his 1967 book *The Ghost in the Machine*,[107] the philosopher and social critic Arthur Koestler introduced the concept of a holon, described as a "whole part." Nothing is separate and nothing is together. Everything is contextualized, nested. Everything flows into everything else, then exits the same way it enters. An atom is part of a molecule, a molecule part of a cell, a cell part of an organ, an organ part of a body, a

body part of a household, a household part of a neighborhood, a neighborhood part of a city, a city part of a state
which, in turn, is part of a nation-state which, in turn, is part
of the geopolitical body politic we call globalization. Up top
there sits the overachievers. The go-getters. The Ivy Leaguers.
Or those born into it, not unlike how a baby beaver is tubu-
larly greased into the caste of its colony.[108] Yet what goes up
must come down. That's the pragmatism of power and policy. Decisions are made by the few that trickle down through
the many, doing so across geographic scales that hierarchi-
cally drift from international edicts to federal laws to state
and local ordinances to street wisdom to hate and love in the
household where it all ultimately lands with a thud into the
geography of the mind and body. It's the ultimate proving
ground of how we are doing.

A tumor. A murmur. An infection. A wheeze. A rash. A
bullet. A syringe. A voice in the head. No voice. A feeling of
hope. Not the feeling of hope. A whimper. A wail. A laugh. A
deep breath. An asphyxiation. These are the outcomes that
matter. We can talk big government v. small government,
Gross Domestic Product, secular stagnation, inflation, bear
markets and bull markets, cryptocurrency and kryptonite,
until we are blue in the face. And we do. America is one big
red, white, and blue avatar that's bloated in its delusion and
uncatchable in its breath, a gurgling made possible by the fact
that we refuse to acknowledge that the term "late capitalism"
is just a proxy for the reality that we've been making shit up
for some time.

A COVID-era *New York Times* headline concedes: "Too
Big to Fail: The Entire Private Sector."[109]

Wait. Come again?

Matter of fact, the discipline of economics may be the foolhardiest endeavor we have ever pretended so hard upon, if only because the discipline's experts, economists, aren't too good at doing the "science" part of the social science discipline. An International Monetary Fund (IMF) study,[110] for instance, analyzed economists' ability to forecast recessions, which is the meteorologist equivalent of predicting hurricanes or the epidemiologist equivalent of predicting pandemics. The IMF researchers appeared to linguistically turn themselves into knots by what they found, concluding that the "forecasts by the private sector and the official sector are virtually identical...both are equally good at missing recessions." So, tied for first in being bad. The IMF study ends by noting "strong booms are also missed, providing suggestive evidence for...the view that behavioral factors — the reluctance to absorb either good or bad news — play a role in the evolution of forecasts."[111]

This "reluctance to absorb either good or bad news" is the opposite of what's supposed to happen. The scientific method is what it is because it privileges the analysts' ability to objectively observe whatever it is that is being considered. No a priori normative judgements are needed. You check your baggage at the door and coolly observe the phenomena as it unfolds in front of you. A hunch takes place. A light bulb goes off. A theory may develop, which is nothing more than an abstraction — a mental model — of a given reality you're paying mind to. Evidence may build to bloom the theory, or it may build so it dies on the vine. Regardless, a body of knowledge is born in either the presence or absence of proof, with neither privileged over the other.

But that's not how discovery happens in practice. Humans are less robotic than animalistic. We wake up, eat oatmeal, and dream big and fear big, and so the mental models we go to work with — and the algorithms that become bricklayered to give them empirical heft — are guard-railed by the hopes and fears that make the human, human. And while that's true of all disciplines, there's arguably no vocational calling more intertwined with the powers that pre-exist than economics, in which the economist is far less an objective discerner of the invisibly-handed market than a participant in the wild kingdom of cash money wherein all partakers are so ravenously engaged in what's happening that they fall limp in the ability to figure out why it's happening. Let alone whether it should be happening at all.

A 2022 *New York Times* expose, for example, entitled "Behind the Scenes, McKinsey Guided Companies at the Center of the Opioid Crisis"[112] detailed how the McKinsey consulting agency deployed their economists and MBA warlocks to turn pharmaceutical companies into legalized drug cartels, selling prescribed heroin pills to America's poorer parts under the cover of supply and demand curves. You know, Pablo Escobar, PhD. The public cost of these economists' PowerPoint presentations has been devastating to America's economy, draining $1.5 trillion from the national coffers via lost productivity and public subsidy in 2020 alone, as uncovered by a 2022 report to the Senate's Joint Economic Committee.[113] The dissonance of it all is incommodious. Or, if you prefer: unsound.

This is to say nothing of the fact that a founding presumption of the field, i.e., homo economicus — which asserts that the agent of the market is the "rational man"[114] — is rubbish.

The world is sick so often. Go look out the window and tell me what you see. Greed is good is more right. This is arguably why economists are so lionized. Not because of their goddamn utility functions. But for the insinuation, or the allusion, (or want) that they hold the keys to the castle. Economists are reputed to know where the loot is. Or, more accurately, where the looting is.

Perhaps it's no surprise, then, that next to every president, senator, governor, congressional representative, mayor, etc. sits an economist, cavernous chest puffed out and squawking, piping up. It's a characteristic self-assurance the profession radiates that keeps the illusion of the field's replicability and cogency intact. "There exists an implicit pecking order among the social sciences," begin the authors of the article "The Superiority of Economists,"[115] "and it seems to be dominated by economics. For starters, economists see themselves at or near the top of the disciplinary hierarchy...as the most scientific of the social sciences."

The danger, here, is not that economists make money selling bullshit transactionally. All disciplines to some extent do that. A plumber does that. The danger is that economists are listened to by powerful people. Or they are told to by powerful people. Moreover, Americans look to economists. They are the high priests of the other religion that we'd been presaged about: "For you say, I am rich," notes the Book of Revelation, "I have prospered, and I need nothing, not realizing that you are wretched, pitiable, poor, blind, and naked."[116] That's fine. That's Gospel. But this is America, 2023. Billionaires are making space forces. Kardashians are made into billionaires. So, you are not naked, blind, poor, pitiable, or wretched. You are just rich. And if you are so then you are so because you fell on the right side of a story that was told, and you believed how it ended. Which is never.

It's 8:45 in the morning. I leave the carousel sliding doors of the cancer hospital and walk out onto the street. There, we sit. Sponges below a broken glass ceiling. Dying the death of a million cuts. I sit on a bench by the Survivor's Garden. It's got a walking path and a bell but never any people in it. It's early springtime. Sunny and cold. I am waiting for my mom to pick me up. I feel like a child. I need to get home to my wife and three kids, but I can't drive anymore. My visual field is cut on my left side from my craniotomy. I could fake it and drive. But that's how we got here in the first place. Everyone skirting their personal responsibility to the collective because it's been drilled into their head that they, the individual, have all the say when, in fact, they have none. Everyone and their phony liberty. The mass shootings and the 2nd Amendment. The mask freak outs and whatever the hell amendment that is. What a mess. What a tale.

In the 2017 paper "Narrative Economics"[117] that would go on to be a best-selling book of the same name, Nobel Laureate, Detroit-born economist Richard Shiller speculates on the causative factors of major economic events, such as recessions; as well as dominant ideologies, like deregulation and privatization that are the backbone of neoliberalism. Shiller breaks pedagogy with his notion that economics is less formed by logic and numbers than emotions and stories. "We have to consider the possibility that sometimes the dominant reason why a recession is severe is related to the prevalence and vividness of certain stories,"[118] Schiller writes, "not the purely economic feedback or multipliers that economists love to model." He goes on to note that "new narratives may be regarded often as causative innovations" that subsequently change the world order. These narratives aren't birthed by conspirators but rather "originate in the mind of a single individual (or a collaboration among a few)." Shiller references fellow economist Joel Mokyr, who called such individuals the "cultural entrepreneur."[119]

Economist Milton Friedman was one such cultural entrepreneur. His 1970 *New York Times* essay aptly titled "The Social Responsibility of Business Is to Increase Its Profits"[120] was the shot heard around the world. The message was deceptively simple, or that CEOs have one master to serve, the shareholders, and they do so by maximizing corporate welfare with little-to-no regard for societal welfare. "The businessmen believe that they are defending free enterprise when they claim that business is not concerned 'merely' with profit but also with promoting desirable 'social' ends," Friedman lashes out, "that business has a 'social conscience' and takes seriously its responsibilities for providing employment, eliminating discrimination, avoiding pollution and whatever else may be the catchwords of the contemporary crop of reformers… Businessmen who talk this way are unwitting puppets of the intellectual forces that have been undermining the basis of a free society these past decades."

Friedman's strawmen of "businessmen who talk this way" was never clarified in his essay, but it didn't matter. The executive class welcomed the message, for it absolved them of many a responsibility outside making money and not acknowledging the Scripture re: Revelation. Nor did it matter that Friedman's ideological stance that profit was purity in a free enterprise system was without solidified evidential merit.[121] Laissez-faire capitalism, the most dominant geopolitical ideology of our time, wasn't modeled in as much as told in. Think of history, then, as not written by victors but by the policymakers who are the best storytellers, or alternatively, by the actors standing in for policymakers who are the best storytellers.

"Viral narratives need some personality and story," Shiller writes in his book *Narrative Economics*.[122] "One such narrative involved movie star Ronald Reagan, who became a household name as the witty and charming character of the highly popular US television show General Electric Theater from 1953 to 1962...Reagan used his celebrity to launch a massive free-markets revolution whose effects...are still with us today."[123]

In his first inaugural address Reagan declared, "In this present crisis, government is not the solution to our problem; government is the problem." Prime Minister Margaret Thatcher would echo his sentiment in more controversial terms: "Who is society? There is no such thing. [N]o government can do anything except through people and people look to themselves first."[124]

What arose was the trickle-down Reagan/Thatcher era defined by a decade's worth of policies that'd demean the public good for the private good. Those policies that were made would carve up the country, selling off its parts like a butcher would cuts of meat. Not inconsequentially, it was a social science consensus that provided the legitimacy for such an ideological stance, one greased into existence through a network of economic consultants who entered boardrooms to present on findings that they pretended were coming from them rather than into them. You've heard the terms. Efficien-

cy as a means and profit as an end. Privatization and deregulation. Automation and off-shoring. You also know the industries: transportation, utilities, manufacturing, corrections,
education, healthcare.

The effect in Cleveland was exemplar: In 1969, 73% of region's income came from salaries and wages. It came from
work. By 2021 that number decreased to 52%. The percent of
Clevelanders' income that came from dividends, interest, and
rent, however, or money paid to stockholders, lenders, and
landowners, went from 14% to 19%. Dubbed "financialization", this is essentially the process of money making money.
The scholar Gerald Epstein defines financialization as "the
increasing role of financial motives, financial markets, financial actors and financial institutions in the operation of the
domestic and international economies."[125] Epstein explains
that the financialization of an economy — historically symp-
tomatic of a declining hegemonic power — is part and parcel
with a shift in money "between capital and labor on the one
hand, and between management and workers on the other
hand." And while I could go on with the finger-wagging statistics, like the top 1% of earners in America took home 19% of
the national income in 2021, up from 10% in 1980,[126] it's akin
to beating a dead horse back to life. That's because stories
matter, not stats. Civilization, after all, was built around a
campfire, not a spreadsheet, as is evidenced in the *Smithsonian Magazine* piece, "How Conversations Around Campfire
Might Have Shaped Human Cognition and Culture."[127]

Unsurprisingly, then, the free market narrative remains
as entrenched in the mythos of America as much as the image
and aura of a pre-cancerous Marlboro Man. The dude. So cool.

Sources of Income in Cleveland Metro, 1969 to 2021

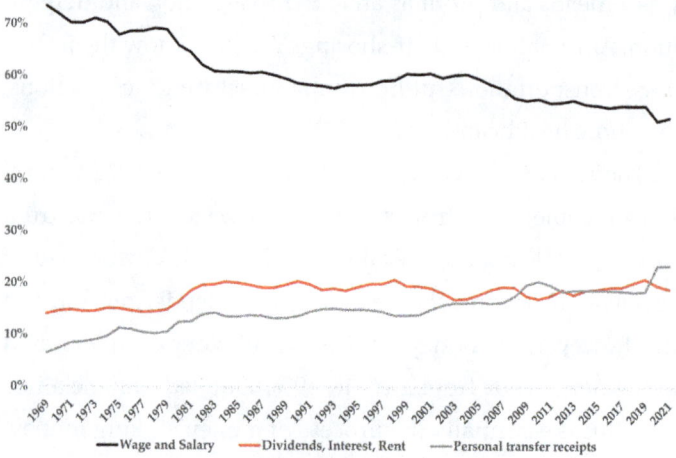

Source: Bureau of Economic Analysis, 1969 to 2021

So rugged. So sans lumps and an electrolarynx. That legend of a hyper-individualistic American Dream persisting like some duct-taped, motionless North Star that offers guidance to life's passersby. Us hitchhikers of the galaxy. Everyone magnetized by the shimmying of self-determination but fewer confiding in the precarity and terror of the direction. That, too, is the essence of power, with the organizational behaviorist and management consultant Jeffrey Pfeffer saying the quiet part out loud, describing power as the "potential ability to influence behavior, to change the course of events, to overcome resistance, and to get people to do things that they would not otherwise do."[128]

But the body doesn't lie. Life expectancy in the U.S. has not only plateaued, it's declined for three consecutive years recently, veering into a trajectory of stalled longevity that's not close to the paths of other modernized nations. In their recent study "Life Expectancy and Mortality Rates in the

United States, 1959–2017,"[129] the authors find that Americans'
life expectancy decline was a function of Americans aged 25
to 64 dying early, *mostly from suicide, overdose, and various or-*
gan system failures. "The notion that U.S. death rates are increasing for working-age adults is particularly disturbing because it is not happening like this in other countries," said
Steven Woolf, the co-author. "This is a distinctly American
phenomenon."[130]

Life expectancy at Birth for G 7 Nations.

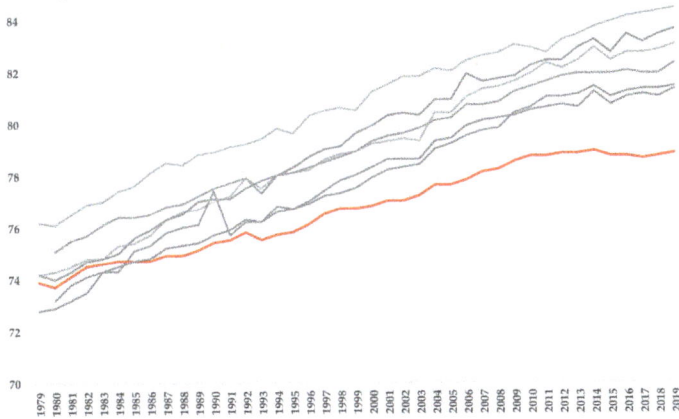

Source: OECD, 1979-2019

Then there's COVID. America has the most COVID
deaths worldwide, nearly double that of second-place Brazil[131].
This is not because we don't have skilled healthcare. It's because what's been sewn has been reaped. "[I]f there is a single
economic policy lesson to learn from the coronavirus pandemic," explains management theorist Roger Martin, "it is that the
United States' obsession with efficiency over the last half century has brutally undermined its capacity to deal with such a

catastrophic event. The virus shows that making our companies efficient also made our country weak."[132] This is clear by
the fact that when the plague smacked into American bodies, it
pushed Americans' wobbling expectancy of living off a cliff.[133]

Life expectancy at Birth for United States

Source: OECD, 1960-2020

It's 9:15 A.M. I'm sick, but I don't yet feel weak. I am in
the car. I leave the part of Cleveland attached to its economic
upswing, or it's medical and cultural district, University Circle, and I enter into its other parts. Houses tilted. Roofs pushed
in. Windows with little light on inside. Those windows part of
a house, the house part of a neighborhood, the neighborhood
part of a city, the city part of a state which, in turn, is part of a
nation-state which, in turn, is part of the geopolitical body
politic. Up there, stories are told. These tales invariably trickle
down, stilling into the geography of our mind and body. Into
organs. Into cells. Into molecules. Into atoms. Into whatever it
is that breaks down into the barrenness that scientists can't
find. We have a galaxy within us, shooting stats that would

shoot out if they were allowed to. I think about these things as I ride shotgun through the city, moving towards the holon of home.

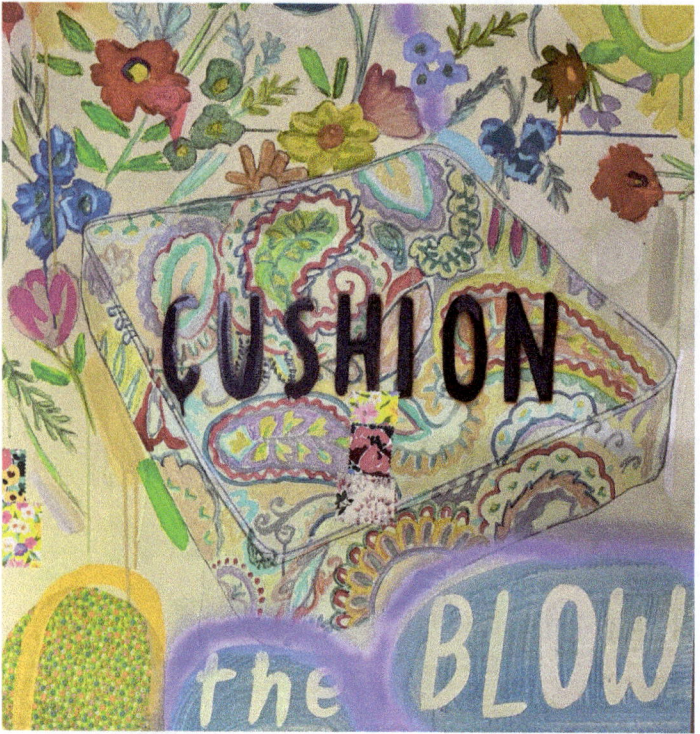

Painting "The Sick Bed"

More Than Fifteen Minutes of Blame

It's all a high-stakes affair now. Letting your hair down means shaving it off. A checkup is essentially a markup of the distance from your presence to the cliff's edge. Down below is where our ancestors are at.

Normalcy died in force the day of my diagnosis. You don't get greased into brain cancer. You get thrown in. Or dropped in. More stork, less birth canal.

There was the time, for instance, when my wife and I had a telemedicine visit with a neurosurgeon in Cleveland. He essentially said my tumor was inoperable. Fine. But his bedside manner was trash. We were a couple stuck in a nightmare, and he was playing the ghoul. Why? I will never know. Nor did I care to ask. Besides, the tumor was not inoperable. 98% was, in fact, removed. Without that surgery, I'd be dead right now. But I am not dead right now. I am alive right now.

This doesn't mean the resection surgery, or the craniotomy, wasn't risky. It involves screws, clamps, and a Gigli saw, the latter of which is a flexible wire saw used by surgeons for bone cutting that, according to *Wikipedia*, is "mainly used for amputation."[134] While rough-sounding, it beats what neurosurgeons used in ancient times. It's a chronology detailed in the *Journal of Neurosurgery* article "How to get in and out of the skull: from tumi to 'hammer and chisel' to the Gigli saw and the osteoplastic flap."[135] The author, Dr. James Goodrich, explains that the earliest anthropological evidence of surgery in *Homo Sapiens* involved the art of drilling holes in the head, dating back to at least 12,000 years Before Christ. "Making 'holes in the skull' is an ancient art and by some is considered the second oldest profession in the world," Goodrich explains, "the first being prostitution.

"Despite these neurosurgical evolutions, lots can go wrong when sawing into the head. But I tried not to overthink it and was successful for the most part. Certain life circumstances are beyond the natural limits of anticipation. This was one of them.

Yet it didn't stop me from trying to commandeer some control over the situation. My thoughts turned to ways to influence my globally-renowned neurosurgeon. Now, neurosurgeons don't lack for confidence. They make heart surgeons look lamblike when it comes to ego exudence. So, nothing I could say or do was going to make him more confident, more focused, steelier, etc. I knew this. But my want was illogical, emotive. If I could get him to recognize that I, too, was aspirational. That I, too, climbed ladders of success. That I was not just a victim. I was not just sick. Who knows? Maybe having a fuller picture of your patient affects the way you slice them up. In fact, I was considered a "public intellectual" in Cleveland, opining on ways the Rust Belt can progress economically, socioeconomically, and social psychologically in numerous interviews, speeches, essays, and reports. The work led to some noticeability. My research and ideas were covered nationally and internationally by the likes of the *CBS Evening News, PBS NewsHour, BBC, CBC, the Los Angeles Times, the New York Times, the New Yorker, Time,* Toronto's *The Globe and Mail, ESPN The Magazine, Sports Illustrated,* among others.[136] Perhaps my favorite bit was bein interviewed for a CBC radio documentary called "In the Shadow of Steel: Hamilton and the search for a new future." It was produced by Mary O'Connell who, in an interview after its airing, described my work as "a cultural writer who's made the idea of the rust-belt his life's work...using terms 'like rust-belt fatalism' and 'rust-belt chic' to frame both reinvention and what's going on in the psyche of those who live in rust-belt cities."[137] I liked that. Anyway, I had my fifteen minutes of fame and then some. How to remind my neurosurgeon of that?

Now, more than ever, I read what the dying have said. A few months after diagnosis I came across a deathbed conversation between philosopher Sam Keen and cultural anthropologist Ernest Becker that was transcribed into a piece entitled "The Heroes of Everyday Life: A theorist of death confronts his own."[138] That theorist was Becker, who was dying of cancer at the age of 49. Several years prior, Becker shot to intellectual fame with the publication of his Pulitzer Prize winning book *The Denial of Death*.[139] In it, he postulates that everything we do is motivated by the need to suppress awareness of our own mortality. "This is the terror," as Becker put it, "to have emerged from nothing, to have a name, consciousness of self, deep inner feelings, an excruciating inner yearning for life and self-expression and with all this yet to die." Is that what happens after death? A deep, oblivious nothingness? An infinite, lukewarm bath in the tub of a cold grave? I don't know. And an A-list of thoughtful philosophers who have attempted to find out didn't exact an answer either. But that's not the point. The key, here, is not the veracity of the fear of death. Fear doesn't need veracity. Rather, it's the veracity of the fear's impact. How does death anxiety live forward in the life of the individual? And how does what's intrapersonal become the interpersonal become the chorus of culture and ultimately the symbols, images, and mythologies that congeal into the god-like a priori backdrop of human experience that C.J. Jung called "the collective unconscious"?[140]

It does so through our actions. These actions can be professional, familial, religious, romantic, or intellectual. On the grandest of scales, examples include Pythagoras' theorem, Ford's assembly line, the harem of Ismail Ibn Sharif, the conversion of Paul the Apostle and his attendant beheading, Einstein's theory of relativity, Ali's shuffle, Morrison's *Song of Solomon*, Didion's *Slouching Toward Bethlehem*, and, of course, Michelangelo's Sistine Chapel.

Beyond acts of creation or self-elevation, behaviors can also veer toward the less sublime. Acts of oppression and persecution, for instance, are also acts of self-relief, if only because there's an illusory measure of a control of oneself through the control of another self. Or other selves. There's been no lack of ink spilled on how the ricochets of horror in World War II flowed from the brittle, terrified, repressed shadow self of Adolf Hitler.[141] The frail masculinity of Putin and its impact on the Ukrainians' ability to breathe comes to mind in recent times. Together these actions—and not just history's "big ones," but also the day-to-day "small ones" (being lost in the rat race and money chase, addiction, etc.)—pool to mold what Becker calls a "character armor" that dulls us of the existential terror that is being alive, yet which also dulls us to the profundity of life's graces. After all, if you can't see, you can't see.

As the interview unfolds—with Becker lying in hospice, a nurse tending to his needs: bringing crushed ice—he reemphasizes his central thesis: that the terror of life is real. "People are really fragile and insecure," Becker says. "This is the truth. There is a beautiful line in the [movie] *The Pawnbroker* where the main character [reflects on his Nazi oppressors] and says 'I couldn't do anything. I couldn't do anything.'[142] We do anything to keep ourselves from the knowledge that there is nothing we can do."[143]

I hated hospitals. But there was nothing I could do. The days of avoiding doctors were mercilessly long gone. My cancer will never remit, so I am told. Treatability means getting to the next year, if not the next month, by all means necessary. Life has become a process of medicalization so as to kick the proverbial can down the proverbial road. But you do what you got to do, you tell yourself. And then you do it. The mind is amazingly resilient in turning what's earth-shattering into the banal. Otherwise, you are just hanging around bridges. Huffing glue.

But I'm not alone. I am part of an online forum where others and their caregivers are in the same headspace and bodyspace as my family and me. They range in age and race and religion and class. But what's uniformly shared is the fact we're all cutting through a brush of fire and thorns, materialized as a terminal illness rooted in the so-called site of consciousness: the brain. Life is a goddamn jungle. It is not a crystal terrain of gumdrops and gravity clocks. But rays of light shine down through the treetops and lay evidence to something else on the ground besides a cut-throated survival leading into the clearing of clarity that is the theoretical physicist's enlightened confusion.

Granted, the internet is often a bullhorn of yuck where people dig in and bitterly offer no concession or compassion. The cacophony of sounds is the worst of us. But this is not how it is in this group of people touched by brain cancer. The forum is filled with words that are equal parts faith, resilience, perseverance, and, yes, dread, grief, anger, and disagreement. This state of affairs disallows the death denial to build up that Becker talked about which, in turn, serves to stomp the bullshit back in its bullshit box. It's a place of solace and inspiration. It's remarkable what the human spirit can muster in the face of everything feared becoming unfeared, if only because one's worst nightmares are there even after waking up. All of us, then, facing, with some semblance of elegance, the archetypal history of humanity's horrors and defeats that've accumulated in the back of the One Mind, or the "Unus Mundus."[144]

"So after almost two years of clear scans learning to use my left side again and having a beautiful baby girl! I recently got the news of regrowth," wrote one middle-aged woman in the brain cancer forum. "I was devastated at first but have had time to process and I still feel confident and in good faith... besides what kind of long-term survivor would I be without a couple of brain surgeries under my belt I'm very thankful for the past two years..."

Wrote a middle-aged man, "I received my surgery and diagnosis 3 weeks ago. After researching GBM I've been struggling with depression and hopelessness. Also lost in a sea of suggestions of alternative treatment options..."

"This is one of the worst diseases there is..." said a younger mother of three. "Knowing the unknown and how quick it can turn is horrific. I come to this group for the brutal honesty. I will never act like this disease is anything but terrible."

Despite being healthy before this—an avid runner—I now firmly exist in the province of the ill. "Everyone who is born holds dual citizenship," writes Susan Sontag in *Illness as Metaphor*, "in the kingdom of the well and in the kingdom of the sick. Although we all prefer to use only the good passport sooner or later each of us is obliged...to identify ourselves as citizens of that other place."[145]

I think about my relative youth and my cancer and what people think about my relative youth and my cancer. This relates to something else Sontag wrote: "Two diseases have been spectacularly, and similarly, encumbered by the trappings of metaphor: tuberculosis and cancer." On cancer, Sontag writes that cancer patients "are lied to and wish to be lied to." "But no one thinks of concealing the truth from a cardiac patient," she continues, "there is nothing shameful about a heart attack. Cancer patients are lied to not just because the disease is (or is thought to be) a death sentence but because it is felt to be obscene—in the original meaning of that word: ill-omened, abominable, disgusting, offensive to the senses."[146]

It was the morning of the surgery, January 19, 2021. I was laying in an ER bed. The surgery got moved up due to my condition deteriorating rapidly. Intracranial pressure was the culprit. I went from talking, to babbling, to unwittingly soundless in a mere few weeks. I was in the ER ICU to get stabilized for surgery and had been there for four days. With Dexamethasone, a corticosteroid, I slowly came to. That morning, I called Andiara, my wife—an immigrant in her 30's from the Rust Belt of Brazil, Minas Gerais, (her dad, Dari, was a steelworker) who had migrated to Cleveland via Florida some 20 years back—and asked her to bring a *Cleveland Plain Dealer* edition from September 2020.[147] On the cover and above the fold there was my piece featured beside a companion piece co-authored by the CEO's of the Cleveland Clinic and University Hospitals, the second of which was my neurosurgeon's boss. I wanted her to bring it so my brain surgeon could see it. The point of my piece was to illuminate the irony of living in a locale, Cleveland, that had great global healthcare but poor local health.[148] In it, I wrote:

Education and health care, or 'eds and meds', have become a globalized industry. Hospitals and universities have taken on the air of worldwide headquarters—or a place in a city, not necessarily of the city. In the case of hospitals, the quality of care is important, but so is a path to more profit. The organizational missions that don't create a beeline to that end can be overlooked. A global hospital, then, can become divorced from its local community, with population health becoming a no-brainer that few people think about.

Photo, Essay in the Plain Dealer.

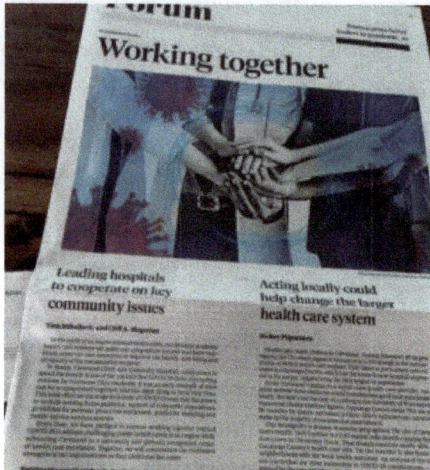

Source: Richey Piiparinen

It was one of my better pieces. And it must've struck a nerve, as the heads of the Cleveland hospitals responded in an admitting manner — their entry paragraph stating plainly: "In the midst of an unprecedented health crisis, our dynamic academic health care systems set aside our competitive natures, and have combined expertise and resources to improve the health, well-being and prosperity of the communities we serve."[149]

It was a mea culpa of sorts, albeit one attempting to wrestle with the twin towers that is record hospital profits on one hand and worsening health outcomes on the other. Cleveland's Cuyahoga County ranks 75th out of 88 counties in health outcomes for Ohio.[150] This, despite Cuyahoga County having the best healthcare in the state. Nationally, the situation is discordant, too. The U.S. has the highest per capita spending on healthcare services, yet it's a loner when it comes to life expectancy among developed nations.[151] Consider it a case of a product becoming divorced from its profession, not unlike a shoemaker not caring about the making of a good shoe. Or a roofer worrying nothing of leaks. An exterminator squeamish of bugs.

Life Expectancy at Birth Vs. Health Spending Per Capita,

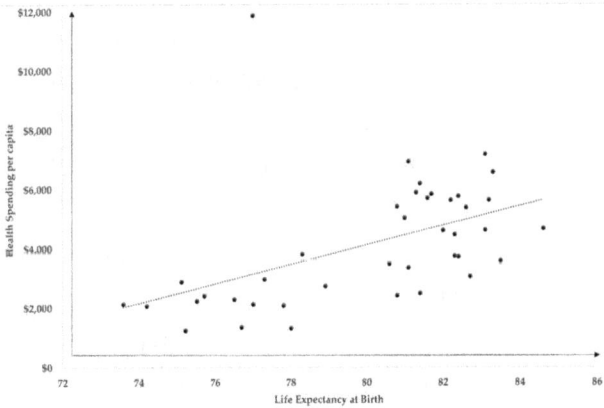

Source, OECD, 2020

How these contradictions formed and then unfolded is a backstory worth touching on. Its CliffsNotes are this: the healthcare industry has been plucked from the poetry of the Hippocratic Oath — e.g., "I swear by Apollo the physician, and Asclepius, and Hygieia and Panacea and all the gods and goddesses as my witnesses, that, according to my ability and judgement, I will keep this Oath and this contract"[152] — to be sucked into the vortex of macroeconomic policy from which the raining of beans has come to be counted by those whose job is to count such things.

As illustrated in the *New York Times'* piece "Reagan, Deregulation and America's Exceptional Rise in Health Care Costs."[153] This happened because it was designed to happen. There's a lot of money to be made in the body. It doesn't turn off, doesn't close, and doesn't stop transacting. There's a 24/7, boundaryless marketplace going on in each of our silhouettes. Why not extract rent?

Such was the thinking that led to the deregulatory movement in the 80's in which investor-owned, shareholder-driven firms became common in healthcare for the first time. They focused on profit maximization, not quality and cost. "No other advanced democracy embraced deregulated health care markets in the way that the U.S. did", explained John McDonough, professor of Public Health Practice at the Harvard Chan School of Public Health. "It swept through health care as it did every other part of the U.S. economy." [154]

While the deregulation of healthcare happened after Ernest Becker's time, it wouldn't have surprised him. All cultures, including their economic systems, are organized around providing possibilities for heroism and the symbolic immortality it provides. "Society has to contrive of some way to allow its citizens to feel heroic,"[155] explained Becker. Money-making is America's biggest sublimation. Fame, or going viral, is second.

Is that good or bad? Keen and Becker reflect on the consequences of shallow reaches. "In your writing," Keen continues in the deathbed confessional, "you stress the need to believe that we are special. You say that we all must be heroes in order to be human." "That is true," Becker responds. "But the important question is how are we to become heroes. Man is an animal that wants to do something about his ephemerality. He wants to overcome and be able to say, 'You see, I've made a contribution to life. I've advanced life, I've beaten death, I've made the world pure.' But this creates an illusion. [Psychoanalyst] Otto Rank put it very beautifully when he said that the dynamic of evil is the attempt to make the world other than it is, to make it what it cannot be, a place free from accident, a place free from impurity, a place free from death."

Perhaps this is why the financialization of healthcare can in particular can feel so soulless. There is nothing more human than coming to terms with the vulnerability of our bodies. Yet there is nothing more transcendent than the urge to go beyond the flesh. To collapse what's sacred into a coin purse is to unleash the profane, and there is arguably nothing more profane in America than how we treat our sick. "In the days before Job, illness was thought to be of divine judgement," Keen goes on, his interview winding down. "If you were sick, it was proof that you were in a state of sin. With the introduction of the naturalistic theory of disease, suffering was severed from guilt. Now, with the advent of psychosomatic medicine, we have brought Job's comforters back to the bedside and we talk about parallels between styles of life and styles of illness. And the cruelest question that is always present, even if unasked, in the presence of illness is: 'Why are you sick?' Or worse yet, 'Why have you done this to yourself?'"[156]

This need to point fingers at the afflicted, it's deeply American. As is the societal pressure for the sufferer to stay hushed about their suffering. This reminds me of two conversations I had soon after my diagnosis. One was with my former group therapist, Dr. Z, a Ukrainian immigrant who ran a few psychiatric hospitals across the State of Ohio. Dr. Z called me on my cell. I hadn't talked to him in years. I explained to Dr. Z that I didn't want to battle a terminal illness in silence. "I see," he said, "but death is a no-fly zone in America." The one thing I will always remember about Dr. Z. is that he'd continuously reference this obscure Russian poem during our group sessions. It's called "Ode to God"[157] and was written by an 18th century poet named Gavriil Romanovich Derzhavin. The part Dr. Z would reference reads:

> *I am the link of all existing worlds,*
> *I am the outer brink of matter,*
> *I am the focal point of living things,*
> *I am the starting place of the divine;*
> *Although my flesh rots into ash,*
> *My mind commands the thunderbolts,*
> *I'm king-I'm slave — I'm worm-I'm God!*

It was the last line that stuck, or the tight juxtaposition of the highest with the lowest. It so uncomfortably fit. For me, it referenced the endless human capacity to hold two competing thoughts in the head simultaneously without the slightest bit of cognitive dissonance. I see it is a source of a lot of our problems. Such as America's sense of collective security requiring everyone to be armed to the teeth.

Around that time, I got a call from a man who is civically active in the State of Ohio. I told him what I told Dr. Z—about not needing to suffer in private. He, too, was hesitant. "Richey, I always thought of you as a humble person," the man said, not uncaringly. "So why do you have to go on bragging you got a brain tumor. It scares the hell out of people. And it is bad for business." His words were not untrue. Brain tumors do scare the hell out of people. And they are bad for business.

Unless your business is brain surgery. The witching hour was approaching. At one point my neurosurgeon came by with a marker to mark an "X" on the right side of my head to denote the correct side of operation. Moments later my wife walked in with the newspaper I requested. I remember the Sunday it came out. Looking at my name besides such "big shots." How proud I was, and it was not necessarily a bad pride. But definitely a pride that was doing me no good at the moment. As I held the paper in my hand and looked at it, discerning it, I saw that it was stained, wrinkled, and most likely germ-ridden. I knew it didn't belong there. There were sanitary reasons, of course. But more than that: It represented a time and place that didn't matter. In this time and place, professional aspirations dawdled beside the unraveling rapid of my less armored life. It was a life where breath supplanted recognition, and where existing was tightly coupled with success.

It was now or never. The hourglass was yawning. I was being gurneyed in, and the Gigli saw was clearing its throat. I kissed my wife goodbye. The look on her face contained the colors and angles of the no-nonsense state of our condition. "Would I ever see you again?" I thought. "Would I ever see you again?" she thought. In between our thoughts was the sound of the surgeons' workshop. Above, the hospital lights hummed and glared. The scalpels were out. I will be laid down, suppled, and excised. I will not have the pen to protect me. I will not be awake to say it's not my fault.

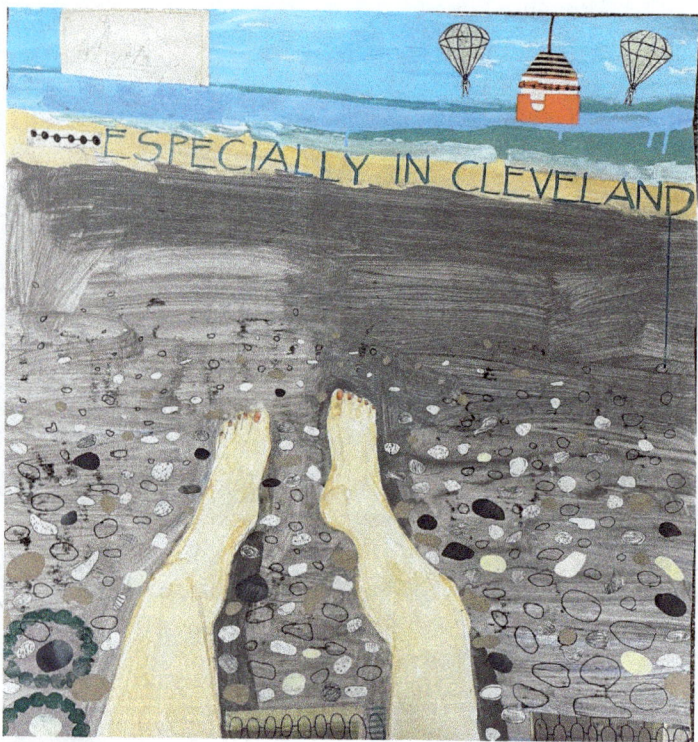

Painting, "A Working Vacation"

Made in the USA:

The Rust Belt

It was the early 1980's and my old street in Cleveland, Colgate Ave., was becoming a shell of itself. By then you didn't have to be well off to join the suburban ranks, barely working class sufficed. We had to stay. My dad was a 2nd District Cleveland cop and there were residency requirements for civil servants. Beyond that, our living arrangements were old school. My dad's mom and brother lived above us, and my mom's mom and dad were across the street. But all around us, families left: the Beckwiths, the Millses, the Davieses. Anger and fear threaded the void.

I remember one time as a child, I was standing on the front porch. It was late summer, dusk. Two White women of Appalachian descent were squaring off in the intersection. Their hands were full of hair. The audience catcalled and moaned. It was a naked display of humanity, an embryonic experience for a child.

Looking back, the scene brought into focus of just how what's big and abstract becomes what's touchable and characteristic of neighborhood decline which, in turn, gets absorbed into thoughts, feelings, and behaviors of everyday people. Every day. In academic parlance, this is what social scientists mean when they say individual outcomes, like health and education, are "socially determined."[158] Elaborating, so much of what's put out there is stored in the mind and body of the observer from where it is urged forward into experience and then on into another's mind and body—making time spent a Jetstream of consequence and dictation.

By 1990 we were gone too. My dad had died. My grandma, his mom, went back to Finland to die. My mom, sister, and I went to the blue-collar suburb of Lakewood. But my mom's mom stayed. One day my grandma, a tough-as-nails, second-generation Italian who drove a boat-long Cadillac and smoked white, skinny cigarettes and drank Pepsi out of a 2-liter, was looking out her living room window at our old house across the street. One man was on the upper front porch, and another was on the lower porch where I once stood watching the women square off. The man higher up shot and killed the man below. Eventually, fists turned to bullets and bruises to death. Emptiness grew. The street became one of phantoms and pieces of fury. Too many Rust Belt streets are like that. If you don't know what I'm talking about, get out, poke around a little bit. If you do, then you do.

You could argue the milieu and mood was warranted. Matter of fact, the American Midwest is known for its Opie-like, oh-geez modesty and plain-speak. Its manners. But there's this kernel within the Heartland—the Great Lakes—and there's a kernel within the Great Lakes—the inner-city Rust Belt—that wasn't born yesterday. That never even touched a turnip truck. That doesn't suffer fools and is only as pleasant as you are. That can cuss with the best of those in South Boston or the Bronx. It's no surprise, then, that the Rust Belt streets can be steeped in acrimony. Irritation was to be expected. Even hate. The sons and daughters of the arsenal of democracy were left to fend for themselves after their lineage split sides and busted knuckles to prove worth and fight fascists. We lionize hard work in America yet dump on the generations of hard workers, setting families up for a pendulum of hard times. America can be so giving and unforgiving. It wasn't fair. Life isn't fair. And what's arguably the most frustrating part about it is that what's unjust is not divinely decreed. There is no such thing as a necessary evil. There are only unnecessary evils. Economic policies and business practices are a bite of the apple. It's all volitional. It's all free choice. Rational man? Yeah, right. "[Y]ou know, there's a difference between the textbook world that economists like to imagine, and the real world where real people have real feelings,"[159] said Paul Romer, a professor of economics at NYU and former Chief Economist at the World Bank. I mean, when one of your high priests speaks so openly dismissive about a backbone of the field, maybe it's time to dress down and stare inquisitively at the curvatures in the mirror and call it like it is.

What's that? It's something that psychologists—be they behavioral, social, existential, or psychodynamic—have known for some time. It's the irrational man that calls the shots. See, for instance, the book from acclaimed economists George Akerlof and Robert Shiller called *Animal Spirits: How Human Psychology Drives the Economy, and Why It Matters for Global Capitalism.*[160] This is one case where you can, in fact, read the book by its cover. From the overview, "The global financial crisis has made it painfully clear that powerful psychological forces are imperiling the wealth of nations today."[161]

To that end, the Rust Belt didn't just happen naturally, like a dead leaf does after falling from a tree. It was manmade and not just the effect of evolutionary market forces. And when I say manmade I am not referring to the construction of things, like a bridge, building, or brick wall. But rather to the composition of decay through avoidance, or what's been dubbed "planned shrinkage," "urban triage," and benign neglect,"[162] which can all be loosely described as the diversion of resources away from places thought of as unworthy of saving. The operative words, here, being "thought of." "Can Buffalo Ever Come Back?" headlined a *Manhattan Institute City Journal* essay by Harvard economist Ed Glaeser back in in 2007.[163] "Probably not," the subheading answered, "and government should stop bribing people to stay there." Womp. Glaeser argues the Feds shouldn't spend money on "resurrecting Buffalo as a place." It's better to help the disadvantaged people that live there. How? By paying Buffalonians to leave. "Urban migrations aren't random," he'd qualify. "America's deserts and mountain ranges aren't densely inhabited for a good reason: few people want to live in such harsh places. Similarly, people and firms are leaving Buffalo for the Sunbelt because the Sunbelt is a warmer, more pleasant, and more productive area to live. The federal government shouldn't be bribing them...to stay in the city."[164]

Granted, demographic trends have been unkind to industrial Midwestern and Great Lakes cities, while they've been bright in the greenfields of the South and Southwest. From 1969 to 2021 the ten largest Sun Belt metropolitan areas grew by 209%, whereas the ten largest Rust Belt metros, including Cleveland, Pittsburgh, and Detroit grew by about 4%. And while recent trends are an echo of economic history, the past persists. Doing so through the act of perception. "Population shrinkage in northern Rust Belt cities has gone on for so long that it is no longer news," begin a pair of commercial real estate investors in a trade webzine recently, "and many investors have simply lost interest in the region."[165] Meanwhile, the "Sun Belt strategy" has become "the standard" in the US property markets, they continue. "Yes, to the Sun Belt. No, to the Rust

Belt—end of story." Yes to Sun. No to Rust. End. Of. Story.

Population Trends 1969 to 2021 Sun Belt vs. Rust Belt,

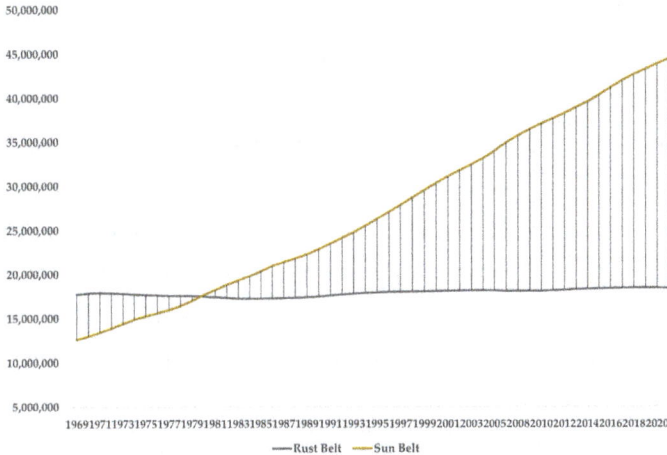

Source: BEA 1969-2021, Author's Calculations

Whether it's a Harvard economist observing an obsoles-
cent Buffalo as buffaloed by the cut-throat paces of comparative advantage and globalization, or a few investor types
stamping the Rust Belt's latest autopsy report, there's little
doubt that perception has a powerful impact in the making
and unmaking of a city's, or a region's, fate. So much of city
building devolves from the processes that comprise the na-
scent and niche field of "psychogeography,"[166] a term that
can be described as the influence emotions have on perceptions and then the subsequent effect each has on behavior.
Behavior, in turn, carves and cuts up the world into pretty
and/or ugly shapes, aesthetics that only further influence
what's perceived and felt. This sets up for a feedback loop
where—in the case of coming and going—losing begets losing and growth begets growth. Or as novelist Philip Roth put

it: "Seeing is believing and believing is knowing and knowing beats unknowing and the unknown."[167] It says here the Rust Belt was partly manufactured by a nation's desirous journey from the unknown into the wannabe known.

As a Junior Senator from Massachusetts, John F. Kennedy penned an *Atlantic* piece in 1954 called "New England and the South" to openly wonder why manufacturing plants were moving from the North to the South.[168] "Nearly 14,000 employees working for the John Doe Company, a New England textile concern, lost their jobs in the period following World War II because of the liquidation of thirteen of their mills," he wrote. The same company suddenly opened a large number of new plants in the South. "Why?" the Senator asks. "To what extent was it influenced by natural advantages...or by the policies of the Federal government?"[169]

What the Senator was insinuating was not insignificant. Governments are not supposed to be in the game of making markets or picking regional winners and losers. That's for the wisdom of market to decide. What's the stuff of this wisdom? In his essay "Mathematical Psychics"[170] published in 1881, F. Y. Edgeworth asserted that "the first principle of Economics is that every agent is actuated only by self-interest." Adam Smith, a founder of modern economic thought, elucidated further, famously evoking the symbolic imagery that a person's innate self-interest, driven by what economists refer to as homo economicus, or "the rational man," serves in aggregate to act as an "invisible hand"[171] that guides the market toward peak efficiency. If everyone knows the art of the deal and everyone gets the best of the deal then that fulfilled, rational self-interest will pool through consumerism and managerial and shareholder want and ultimately fill up and spill over into a pooled public good.

Consider both Edgeworth and Smith early sermonizers of what'd become a moralism that undergirded the rugged individualist mythology that still holds firm in America. "Every individual," Smith writes in *The Inquiry into the Nature and Causes of the Wealth of Nations*, "neither intends to promote the public interest, nor knows how much he is promoting it... he intends only his own security; and by directing that industry in such a manner as its produce may be of the greatest value, he intends only his own gain, and he is in this, as in many other cases, led by an invisible hand to promote an end which was no part of his intention."[172]   Perhaps tellingly, this isn't exactly an inspiring take on the everlasting notion of man and woman's search for transcendence, belonging, and meaning. Contrast Smith's sentiments, for example, with Christian theology, such as Philippians 2:4, "Do nothing out of selfish ambition or empty pride, but in humility consider others more important than yourselves. Each of you should look not only to your own interests, but also to the interests of others."[173]

These messages couldn't be any more discordant, despite arguably being the two ingrown pillars of Americanism: Currency and Christianity. It's no wonder, then, this country is splitting at the seams. Too much discordance equals a wrecked bag of marbles that spills onto the hoedown floor and then the shenanigans that ensues. Regardless, it's hard to overstate just how much the concept of the invisible hand and the wisdom of the market is so nestled into the American way, and the resultant impact these beliefs have on who we are individually and collectively. It's likewise hard to overstate how little empirical evidence there is for its legitimacy[174]. As noted by former Italian ministry of state Laura Pennacchi in her 2021 essay, "Does it make sense to question the morality of capitalism?", [175] an increasing number of economists, like Nobel prizewinner Amartya Sen, have debunked the foundational notion that the glue that holds the global marketplace together is an isolated economic agent that's exclusively self-interested, with Sen branding such an agent a "rational fool" and a "social idiot."[176]

But no amount of reflecting, genuflecting, and finger pointing has been able to reconfigure what market capitalism has become equated with: profit maximization. "I have ways of making money that you know nothing of,"[177] said Cleveland-native John D. Rockefeller. One standard way Rockefeller made profit was to employ a profiteering strategy common to not only industrialists but to execs and shareholders of all stripes: squeeze higher productivity from labor at lower cost of labor for better margins on sales. The framework for this has-cake-and-eats-it-too logic is something called "general equilibrium", in which the invisibly-handed market will push up competition to lower cost of production but not at the expense of product quality.[178]

Relatedly, the most frequented narrative for Rust Belt decline is that the unions got in the way of this market metabolism. Here, the union patronage system constipated the process of equilibrium, leading to higher costs, less productivity, and lower quality. That patronage, then, deterred investment and innovation, inevitably leading to obsoleteness not only at the level of the firm and its product, but also at the level of a regional economy, i.e., the collection of firms in a specific industry in a given time and place. Northern execs, the mantra goes, had no choice but to go to union-less land. Modern-day economists agreed. "We argue that the Rust Belt declined in large part due to a lack of competition in labor and output markets in its most prominent industries, such as steel, automobile and rubber manufacturing," explains a 2013 study called "The Decline of the U.S. Rust Belt: A Macroeconomic Analysis."[179] "The lack of competition in labor markets was closely linked to the behavior of powerful labor unions that dominated the majority of the Rust Belt's manufacturing industries...which led to a movement of economic activity out of the Rust Belt and into...the 'Sun Belt' in the U.S. South."[180]

Missing from their model, however, was the fact that government actively disinvested in the Rust Belt for existential, geopolitical reasons that went way beyond the distaste for collective bargaining. Simply, industrialization was to be had in the Sun Belt. Disinvestment was to be had in the Rust Belt. "And that's that," as the Mob boss who whacked Tommy in *Goodfellas* put it right after the execution.[181]

Life is complicated. Yet there are basic rules that govern our shared existence, like an apple falling from a tree is gravity. Such physical laws secure a needed expectation of how the world works. Dealing with perceptions and feelings, though, is less predictive. Yet how we deal with the unpredictability of what's perceived and felt is fairly predictable. If a thing evokes fear or anxiety, we fight or flee it. If a thing evokes security or aspiration, we go to it. This, in a nutshell, is the story of American sprawl, and not just the migration of people and jobs from big cities into their respective suburbs, but from the cramped, smoked urban geometries of the Northeast and Midwest into the sun-parched greenfields that became America's own suburb: The Sun Belt.

Leaving has always been the best offered solution to American decline. Americans, as Tocqueville noted, "are infamously restless. The recollection of the shortness of life is a constant spur to him. Besides the good things that he possesses, he every instant fancies a thousand others that death will prevent him from trying if he does not try them soon. ..."[182] This hunt for possession and standing led Tocqueville to conclude the American needed things as if they were "never to die". But Americans do die. The father of American psychology, William James, dubbed this all-too-unconfronted, yet all-absorbing reality, "the worm at the core."[183] Yet it's a squirm that's dealt with superficially. "He clutches everything," Tocqueville continued, "he holds nothing fast, but soon loosens his grasp to pursue fresh gratifications. In the United States a man builds a house in which to spend his old age, and he sells it before the roof is on..."[184] A conversation in the 1950s "sitcom suburb" *Leave it to Beaver* self-mockingly demonstrates this self-soothing, if fidgety, state of mind.[185]

> *June Cleaver: "Listen to this house for sale — it sounds perfect for us. 'Charming, three bedroom and den, on beautifully landscaped grounds. Modern dream kitchen. Patio, spacious, airy. The ultimate in suburban living. Near schools and transportation.'"*
>
> *Ward Cleaver: "That's our house dear. They told me they were advertising it this weekend."*
>
> *June Cleaver: "Sounds almost too good to leave."*

That Tocqueville used the example of house hunting to prove his point is not coincidental. The home is peak expression of aspiration and security, and suburbia became the collective symbol of that expression. In 1950, a quarter of Americans lived in the suburbs. A decade later America was split three-ways between suburban, urban, and rural. Suburbanites finally became the dominant residential demographic in 1990.[186] All civilizations have their immortality projects, noted cultural anthropologist Ernest Becker.[187] The Egyptians, for instance, built the pyramids. The Americans built the suburbs.

Not surprisingly, private interests, particularly real estate developers, were keen to noodle that gnaw of the void, promising to fill it. In the 1920s Cleveland's first planned community, Shaker Village, was dubbed a "forever home," with one pamphlet touting the place as "large enough to be self-contained and self-sufficient. No matter what changes time may bring around it, no matter what waves of commercialism may beat upon its border, Shaker Village is secure … protected for all time."[188] Today, the suburban sales pitch is little different. "Personal security in a time of economic and social uncertainty is a very salable commodity," noted a piece in the *Atlantic*.[189] "Developers are not selling security but a sense of security."

After World War II, security was very much on the minds of America's policymakers. The 1950s ushered in "an age of anxiety."[190] It wasn't supposed to be this way. The fascists were defeated. The economy was humming. But a new threat took hold, that of annihilation at the hands of the Soviets. This menace hung like a pall over the American mood. The day after Hiroshima, Hanson Baldwin, the military correspondent to the *New York Times*, wrote "yesterday man unleashed the atom to destroy man, and another chapter in human history opened, a chapter in which the weird, the strange, the horrible becomes the trite and obvious."[191] The psychodrama that would unfold wasn't relegated to the political arena bounded by McCarthyism. It also played out as a national defense policy that'd ultimately help dictate the fate of places, particularly the Sun Belt and the Rust Belt.

Chiefly, there would be an intentional dispersal of population and industry away from older, industrial cities, so notes the author of "The Reduction of Urban Vulnerability: Revisiting 1950s American Suburbanization as Civil Defense."[192] One of the first proposals to argue for decentralization-as-defense came in a 1946 paper called "Dispersal of Cities and Industries."[193] The title says it all. One of the authors was atomic physicist Edward Teller, father of the "H-bomb." "In an atomic war, congested cities would become deathtraps," Teller and his colleagues wrote, arguing that while dispersal would be costly and change the way people live, it was a needed form of protection. Famed science fiction writer of the time, Robert Heinlein, took the rhetoric a step further. In the essay "The Last Days of the United States,"[194] he urged his readers to acknowledge the "true meaning of atomic weapons." Security was an illusion. The distance of oceans no longer mattered. He advocated for a dispersion program that would "spread ourselves so thin that we will be too expensive and too difficult to destroy."

Not all were on board with this plan. Many leaders saw the incentivizing of decentralization as deterministic and in opposition to American individualism. The government would also be picking winners and losers by tilting the playing field of investment toward the South and West. "In the free world, a dispersal program would lead to excessive political controls and curtail our individual liberties and freedoms," argued American defense policy expert Fred Ikle'.[195] Echoing caution was physicist Ralph Lapp in his book *Must We Hide?*[196] Lapp predicted the American people would react "vigorously against any attempt to force decentralization."[197] Lapp's colleagues shared his concern. In a conference conducted by the Industrial College of Armed Services in the early 50s, the debate centered on how the government can direct a dispersal of citizens and private companies out of cities, when the laws of the land supposedly protected against such authoritarian intrusions.

The debates, however, were arguably window dressing. The real debate was about the sell, not whether the product was going to be sold. One presenter at the conference described the solution to the conundrum plainly: the dispersal plan must be explained and sold to Americans. "In a democratic system, political action follows the will of the people," the presenter said. "Our leaders are followers instead of molders of public opinion. Our political leadership is most concerned with doing what the people want, rather than telling them what to do...But in the history of our fair country, if ever public opinion needed molding it is now...This involves telling the people, predicting what they want, and taking action before the crisis is upon us."[198]

Ultimately, this meant bringing American urban planners and economists into the debate. In a 1951 report called "The

Need for Industrial Dispersal" by the Joint Committee on the Economic Report, the authors go beyond the decentralization-as-defense argument to make the case that decentralization was economic development.[199] An excerpt from the report explains:

> *The economy of the United States is facing for the first time in modern history the-possibility of having to maintain industrial production under conditions of direct military action. Coupled with this need for preparing against actual enemy attack is the equally serious problem which is introduced by a permanent large-scale mobilization begun in a period when our existing industrial capacity was fully taken up by civilian demand. Fortunately, the solution of these two problems may well lie in the same direction. Since there is no known defense against the atomic bomb itself except space, dispersion is one of the first considerations for strategic safety of industrial facilities. As labor supply and plant facilities become exhausted in more and more metropolitan areas, it is equally apparent that business is expanding to meet defense-production needs and must look to areas which are not now developed industrially.* [200]

To determine areas that would be actively decentralized for areas into which industry and workers would be coaxed, the report uses the statistic ratio of population to manufacturing employment. Areas in the Northeast and Midwest would be hit hard. That's where manufacturing work was concentrated. Where would industry go? A map from the report is telling. It shows areas where low-income farmers resided: a proxy for a surplus of non-unionized labor. Many of these areas, like Texas, South Carolina, Tennessee, and Georgia, would be targeted for redistribution of money and jobs from the North. It is essentially a map of the Southern Sun Belt, with Appalachia the exception. Those areas were chosen for tax amortization certificates that'd ultimately allow companies to build facilities and buy machinery on the taxpayer's dime.

Map of Targets for Investment

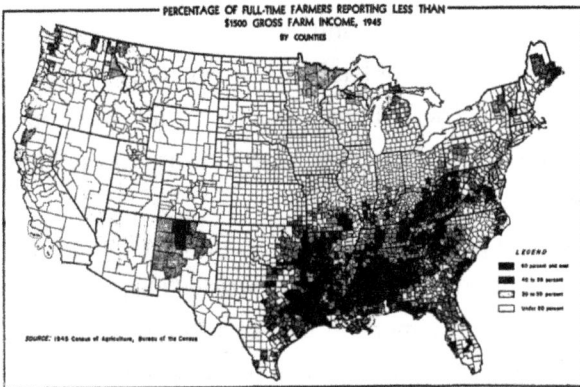

Source: The Joint Committee on the Economic Report, 1951

One concern of decentralization advocates was whether or not people would follow jobs. Will the blue-collar grits from the Northeast and Great Lakes adopt a slower, more sprawling lifestyle? The question was in some respects immaterial. In regards to suburbanization, demand wasn't so much fueling supply as supply was fueling demand. Because while the aesthetic of suburbia and its plotted gardens and picketed fences evoked a sense of security that was undoubtedly bought into by the American consumer, people were going to go where houses were built, regardless. Avoided was the city with its congestion, stink, and decay. Its Sons of Sam and Night Stalkers and "Brooklyn is Burning" and burning rivers. What the consumer desired, noted building consultant Edward Clark, was the comfort and convenience of the suburban ranch complete with its "low silhouette that disappeared into the landscape."[201] Echoed Michigan State sociologist Leo F. Schnore in 1957: "The choices of building sites are made by contractors, real estate operators, and others, notably those involved in the initial capitalization of new developments. Families and individuals are not decisive agents in the process of land-use conversion." [202] But urban planners were. The H Bomb designer Ralph E. Lapp commented that the civil defense strategy was "in the hands of the urban planners."[203]

One such planner was former American Planning President Tracy Augur who, in a 1948 article "Dispersal is Good Business,"[204] said American cities had become "congested and decayed" and that dispersal must be national in scope and not "merely local to a few enlightened areas." These words were a continuation of a 1946 speech in which Augur exclaimed that "the threat of an atom bombing may prove a useful spurt to jolt us forward" toward a standard of development that was spread out and not packed in;[205] or the greenfield and not the brownfield. Auger would go on to be a leading voice in the subsequent urban renewal movement that ultimately meant the wholesale destruction of communities in America's urban centers via the creation of highways that would sever the urban fabric.[206]

When it comes to residential funneling, it couldn't have been done without federal legislation that'd not only apply to the Housing and Home Finance Agency but also the Veterans Administration and the Federal Housing Authority

(FHA). This included the FHA increasing its mortgage insurance authorizations by $1.5 billion in 1954—a figure equaling $15.7 billion in 2022, according to government inflation calculators. It was an amount that the nation's builders openly thanked Congress for in its "aid to private business."[207]

Looking back, it's amazing what this country can do when select, "rational" self-interests coalesce. Whole regions can be rebirthed. The Dixie South, after all, had its own perception problems in the early 20th century. Before its rebranding as the Sun Belt, it was the Cotton Belt: a label with a direct lineage to slavery and Jim Crow. To American intellectuals, the Cotton Belt equaled an "underdeveloped...and native-born southern population" that ran a "backward" economy, so notes Katherine Rye Jewell, author of the book *Dollars for Dixie*.[208] But via the visible hand that was the making of markets, federal policy mountains were moved and realities were rewritten. What was backward became forward and what was forward became backward.

What's new becomes old and what's old new. That's not revelatory. Or bombastic. It's a fact of life. The leaf dies after falling from the tree and crinkles into smithereens after getting marched on by dogs and their owners and school children running to and from class. The dead leaf becomes dust that gets blown into other dust and then the dust unto dust gets lowered into the inseminating ground. A new leaf sprouts on the twig that was the dead one's cradle. And as it is for seasons so it is for the trajectory of cities and their respective regions. Nothing is exempt from the reality of what is. Particularly truth being truth and myth being myth. Lies are lies. Even if they make you feel faux good. Or secure, falsely. And angry, righteously. In the 2019 *New York Times* piece "It's the End of California as We Know It,"[209] the columnist and native Sun Belter Farhad Manjoo explains that California feels "stuck." "We are BlackBerry after the iPhone, Blockbuster after Netflix," he writes. Manjoo explains the region was conceived on so many wrongs: an unsustainable, sprawling design; an inequity-fostering tech-centric economy, a hyper-individualistic culture. "The founding idea of this place is infinitude — mile after endless mile of cute houses connected by freeways and uninsulated power lines stretching out far into the forested hills. Our whole way of life is built on a series of myths — the myth of endless space, endless fuel, endless water, endless optimism, endless outward reach and endless free parking. One by one, those myths are bursting into flame."

Even the investor types are smelling the salts. "In 2020, the US experienced a record-breaking hurricane season..." begin the authors of the article "Tightening the Belts: Rethinking Sun Vs. Rust." "There are and will be larger storms, more often, and the records continue to be broken. The more frequent these events, the less of an advantage the Sun Belt has, and the more the Water Belt is positioned for in-migration and growth."[210] "California appears to be on the verge of a new demographic era," echoes a 2022 report out of the Public Policy of Institute of California, "one in which population declines characterize the state."[211] The sun rises. The sun sets. Vacations begin but inevitably end. There's work to be done. The Rust Belt works. And while that's not sexy and that's not fun...It's not nothing. After all, daiquiris don't grow on trees. How the worm at the core turns.

Painting "Return to Baseline, Return to Blue"

Rust Belt Shame

In a June 15th, 1981 *Time* magazine puff piece called "Nothing Rotten about the Big Plum," the author describes how then-Mayor of Cleveland, George Voinovich, sauntered onto the mound at Municipal Stadium wearing a t-shirt emblazoned with Cleveland's new marketing campaign, "New York's the Big Apple, But Cleveland's a Plum."[212] Perhaps predictably, Voinovich then proceeded to throw out the "first plum,", a play off the ceremonial first pitch. Unlike a baseball, however, a plum will splat. Which it did in this case. In the catcher's mitt. The Yakety sax-like scene illustrates the lengths cities will go to project an image as far away from reality as possible. These city branding campaigns usually end poorly.

Mayor Voinovich throws out of the first plum.

Source: David I. Andersen

Meanwhile, in Pittsburgh the city's marketing elite leaned in with a character called Border Guard Bob. Dan Fitzpatrick, a reporter for the Post-Gazette, explained that Border Guard Bob was a fictional Barney Fife-type persona who was to star in a television ad and be put on billboards. "The idea was for Border Guard Bob to wear a uniform and stop young people at Western Pennsylvania's borders," he wrote, "before they had a chance to leave for other cities. If he was unable to persuade people to stay, Border Guard Bob would have hitched a bungee cord to the car's back bumper and, looking into the camera, say: 'He'll be back.'"[213] Yikes.

Where does the will, or lack of will, come from that incites these once-powerhouse cities to so pitifully delude themselves into thinking that this is how to put yourself out there? How does a collective devolve to be so vulnerably self-unawares?

Though my career is in the field of city building, particularly urban theory and policy, my initial graduate training was in clinical psychology. My thesis was on secondhand, or vicarious, trauma related to the September 11th attacks, which turned into a few published studies with titles like "Stress Symptoms of Two Groups Before and After the Terrorist Attacks of 9/11/01" in places like *Perceptual and Motor Skills*.[214] The broader ramifications of the findings are that collectives, such as nations, cities, or neighborhoods, are impacted by experiences on an aggregate level just as individuals are on a personal level. Collectively, the perceptual catch of these experiences—be they traumatically and instantaneously profound like 9/11, or slower-moving and distress-inducing like deindustrialization and the job and income losses and communal, familial, and personal conflicts that inevitably follow—become absorbed as memories of what was, what is, and what may never be. These memories, however, often remain below the level of conscious awareness. They are thus not processed but left undigested, not unlike a brick of food in the belly that echoes forward in the tainting of future experience via the prism of emotional distress, else emotionlessness. In other words, loss unfelt is loss everlasting.

"Only echoes answer me,"[215] writes the playwright Anton Chekhov in *Swan Song*, the quote referencing the extent of how things can unravel like a fountain of bits and pieces, the display of which is breakage flowing into breakage. Or as Yeats put it in the poem "The Second Coming:"[216]

> *Turning and turning in the widening gyre*
> *The falcon cannot hear the falconer;*
> *Things fall apart; the centre cannot hold;*
> *Mere anarchy is loosed upon the world,*
> *The blood-dimmed tide is loosed, and everywhere*
> *The ceremony of innocence is drowned;*
> *The best lack all conviction, while the worst*
> *Are full of passionate intensity*

The issue, then, for people, and groups of people, i.e., cities, isn't about whether things fall apart—things will fall apart—but what's to be done with the remains. Will they be ignored while yet another undoing is in the making? This seems the approach humanity is taking toward climate change, late capitalism, and disinformation. Or will they be leveled with and carried forward?

Arguably, the Rockstar of the notion that collectives have

thoughts and feelings is sociologist Émile Durkheim, who formulated the idea of a "collective conscience," a concept described in his 1893 book *The Division of Labor* in Society as the "totality of beliefs and sentiments common to the average members of a society."[217] The focus, here, is on the specific beliefs and sentiments about the geography of the Rust Belt that arrive as projected judgment from the outside in yet are preserved by a peculiar regional flare for the self-own that operates from the inside out, the latter of which I've come to call "Rust Belt Shame."[218]

It's important, here, to delineate shame from other negative affect, particularly guilt. Guilt is about an act done and the consequences of one's conscience. "I feel bad. I have done wrong." These are the types of words we hear in our head when feeling guilty, and it's is an Adam- and Eve-like self-discourse arising from the backlash that is a moral authority. "Then the Lord God said to the woman, 'What is this you have done?' And the woman said, 'The serpent deceived me, and I ate'."[219]

Shame is different. If guilt is the internal feeling Adam and Eve felt as they left the Garden of Eden, then shame is the feeling they felt from the hisses of the onlookers that watched from the balcony of biblical context. In modern-day parlance, shame is the gas that gets you cancelled. But hive-minded morality chutes can lead society astray, especially if they are constructed from a collective conscience that is more repressed than processed. Or more virtue signaling than virtuous. As a guiding, resolving, feeling shame carries with it a lot of baggage. "Shame is a soul eating emotion," noted psychoanalyst C.G. Jung,[220] referencing shame's groupthink tendency to try and erode what's wrong instead of grow what's right. And it's an emotional self-tunneling that can lead to a house of mirrors as far as not knowing where progress proceeds from, a reality eloquated supremely in Antoine de Saint-Exupéry's, *The Little Prince.* "Why are you drinking? demanded the little prince. "So that I may forget," replied the tippler. "Forget what?" inquired the little prince, who was already sorry for him. "Forget that I am ashamed," the tippler confessed, hanging his head. "Ashamed of what?" insisted the little prince, who wanted to help him. "Ashamed of drinking!"[221]

Or in this case: "Why are you ashamed, Cleveland? Because I am a plum. Why are you marketing yourself as a plum? Because I am ashamed."

That shame is a particularly important sentiment which clots in the Rust Belt conscience, and it's the tributary so many Rust Belters flow into and out of in this stream of living that's been labeled "flyover country," what's the source emotion, or the experiential watershed, that gives Rust Belt Shame its materiality? It's most basic element, its ground truth, is loss, chiefly the loss of status. Here, Lao Tzu put it best: "Pride attaches undue importance to the superiority of one's status in the eyes of others." And shame is fear of humiliation at one's inferior status in the estimation of others."[222] Legendary sociologist Charles Cooley theorized in 1922 that there were essentially only two social emotions, pride and shame. "The thing that moves us to pride or shame," Cooley wrote, "is not the mere mechanical reflection of ourselves, *but an imputed sentiment,* the imagined effect of this reflection upon another's mind."[223]

The Rust Belt, of course, is not alone here. Cities the world over are afflicted with the hangovers of history. "Nearly every historic city has its brand of melancholy indelibly associated with it," begins the author of the essay "From the "Geography of Melancholy"; in the *American Reader*, "each variety linked to the scars the city bears. Lisbon has its saudade: a feeling of aimless loss tied to the city's legacy of vanishing seafarers, explorers shipwrecked in search of Western horizons. Istanbul has huzun: a religiously-tinged brand of melancholy rooted in the city's nostalgia for its glorious past."[224] But the Rust Belt's version seems to go beyond the romantic notion of nostalgic longing for better times and into the Japanese art of self-impaling, or Seppuku, known as "hara-kari" in the West.[225] If not for a strange, if subconscious, tendency for the self-dig, how else would you explain selling Barney Fife as a prison guard as the star of an attraction campaign to retain the city's younger, creative types? The whole concept is perverse. Like selling sand to the thirsty.

A few years back, I got contacted by Benjamin Wallace-Wells, a writer for *The New Yorker*, about a piece I wrote in *Belt Magazine* called "Why the Rust Belt is not a Pejorative," that discussed the self-flagellating tendencies found in Cleveland and the rest of the Rust Belt. "Shit happened," I wrote.[226] "Shit is still happening." My point was that a fall from grace had occurred. Deindustrialization and urban core abandonment were real and long-shadowed. Cleveland shrank. It shriveled. As did Pittsburgh, Buffalo, and Detroit. Flint, Youngstown, Erie. Socioeconomic effects ensued. A colossal housing market collapsed. A new settlement pattern was categorized, called the "shrinking city,"[227] and a novel urban aesthetic was even birthed: "ruin porn,"[228] referring to the predilection of vacancy gawkers to play on the untaken cathedrals of the Industrial Revolution. And that it all occurred—the leaving, the shrinking, the decay, the return to earth, in fact all those features of bodily mortality—it triggered a projection in America's mind's eye that something was wrong with "them" but not necessarily with "us."

That's because it's soothing for a collective to compartmentalize its failing parts. To jersey-barrier the appendages vanishing on the vine. And for good reason, because while swaths of the inland were failing, the Sun Belt was growing. The Coasts prospered. New York was New York, never sleeping. Las Vegas was shiningly gluttonous, albeit being literally and figuratively built on a house of cards. Matter of fact, it can be argued that the Rust Belt was the first geography in modern America to "die"; that is, not grow. There was the Old West and its ghost towns, but the Old West never held such a prominent position in the American hierarchy as did the Arsenal of Democracy—home to the likes of Rockefeller, Carnegie, Mellon, and Ford. And given America is a manifest-destined country whose soul was conceived on the crossroads of unbridled consumption and growth, the side-eyed glances, the head shakes, the laughs at that kept coming from late night talk shows at a region that was named after a loss of gloss, well, it was not unexpected. American exceptionalism wasn't conceived to expire. That would make it unexceptional. So, mock the loss and tend to growth. Mock reality and make myth. Drink a boat drink and play roulette. For it's all uphill from here.

Still, the projections, the Cleveland jokes, they are one thing. That's punches taken. But why do we as a people accept it, let alone curate it? "I have, in fact, never lived in a place whose proud residents so consistently and gleefully disrespect their hometown as Cleveland," notes well-known Jeopardy champ Arthur Cho in his Daily Beast piece "Cleveland Comes Crawling Back to LeBron: The Masochism of Rust Belt Chic."[229] Cho, a Cleveland transplant, goes on to write that though he hates to "engage in victim-blaming," the reason "everyone dogs on Cleveland is that we ask for it." Why? Cho concludes: "If we weren't suffering, we wouldn't be Cleveland anymore."[230]

Beyond shared identity, there's an adaptive reason for Rust Belt Shame. It's not just a collective phenomenon. It's not simply about losing out on some kind of civic pride arms race measured in skyscrapers, population growth, and Fortune 500's. No, losing one's livelihood and one's ability to make meaning and have value is deeply personal. "This isn't my first rodeo," explained a GM Lordstown plant worker in a 2018 *Guardian* piece, "A 'kick in the stomach': massive GM layoffs leave workers distraught."[231] "This is my third GM plant," the worker continued. "I'd like to be able to plant my roots somewhere. I feel like a gypsy."[232] "This is devastating. This is our livelihood," echoed a co-worker. These public-but-private happenings, then, get stitched into a shared experience that becomes cultural, or part of the menu of sentiments defining a Rust Belt daily life. This response, however, is often adaptive. It's not moaning. "[T]he very fact that shame is an isolating experience also means that if one can find ways of sharing and communicating it this communication can bring about particular closeness with other persons," so notes the author of "Shame and the Social Bond."[233] Hence, the collective character armor that is Rust Belt Shame.

This doesn't mean, though, that such a group identity can't tip from adaptive to maladaptive. Or from digested and transcended to imputed, identity-defining, and welded in place. Which brings us back to *The New Yorker* reporter I noted earlier in this essay. A few days after we talked he wrote a piece entitled "Donald Trump and the Idea of the Rust Belt." From our discussion, the reporter, Wallace-Wells, fittingly latched onto the notion that in the national discourse of the Rust Belt there was—beyond macroeconomic explanations for deindustrialization and the ideological voting proclivities of alienated and angry Reagan Democrats—a depth of the narrative that wasn't exposed and rarely, if ever, discussed. I called this concealed reality "the idea of the Rust Belt," or a worm at the core in the national psyche that's carried around like a shadow that's barely noticed but constantly cast. Wallace-Wells explained that the "idea of the Rust Belt" is a projected upon reality that "...everyone is vulnerable. The story that is told is about the certainty of loss."[234] Yet he also lamented the fact that in that process of existential displacement onto the region, a parallel, story-of-origin has been left out. "It's a little strange to remember the ideas of the Midwest that the Rust Belt has was crowded out," he writes. "The conviction that the heartland provided a moral counterweight to coastal excess and cynicism." He'd go on to reference a Jonathan Franzen interview wherein the author remarked: "There is a prolongation of innocence there, a prolongation of childhood, that has to do with the Midwest being just a little bit farther from the rest of the world."[235] "There is what would strike many Americans as a bizarre absence of cynicism in the room," echoed the writer David Foster Wallace.[236]

Over-romanticized takes? Perhaps. There's lots of ache here. Lots of forfeiture. But that's heaps of places. Show me a place without hurt and I'll show you a powder keg. Either that or a golf cart community. Or both.[237] As for the future of the Rust Belt? There are really only two directions for the region to proceed from, not only from a collective conscience standpoint but also the associated response that is city leadership, policy making, and, of course, city branding. There's the direction that is away from shame and loss. And there's the direction that is through shame and loss. The former gets you a bungee cord hooked up to your belt loop in which you are snatched from the horizon and slung back to baseline: that Sisyphean existence. The latter gets you room to know who you are versus what you are told you are, or what you wrongly tell yourself.

Like you're a plum.

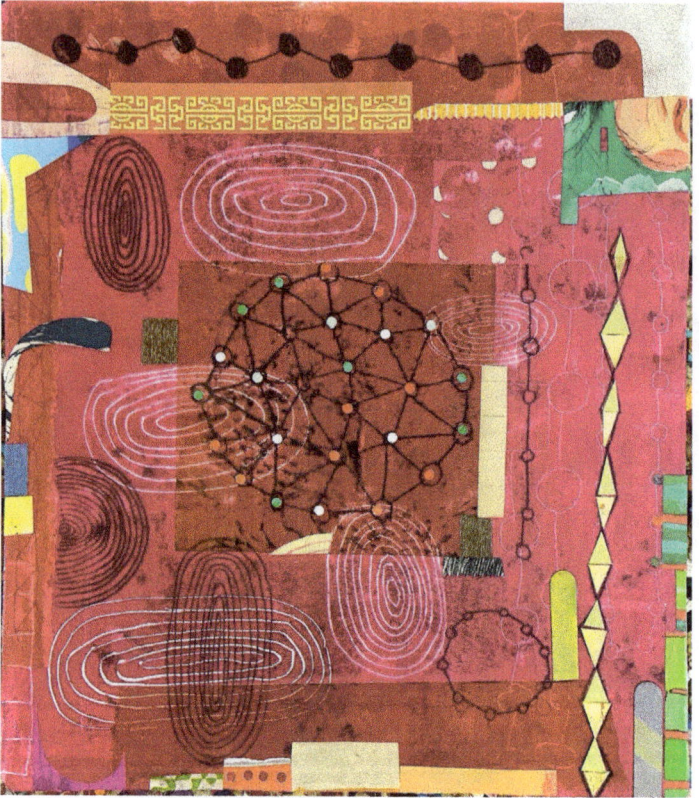
Mixed Media Print Collage "In the Flesh"

Octopus
Hunting

I was in the Chicago suburbs at a kid's birthday party. A fit, older man was before me in tears. I didn't know him well, but I knew him. And I knew what he was saying when he said, "What happened to you, it is terrible." He was speaking about my brain cancer diagnosis. Now, people generally don't know what to say to the incurably ill, and that's no one's fault. There are no natural responses to too-natural situations. Still, when folks refer to the situation as "a thing that happened to me," well, it makes me itch. For it removes me from my fate and exempts me from my evolution. Nothing happened to me. It happened with me. If not from me. This is that story.

When I was five I was kneeling on the second step of a neighbor's back porch petting a black Great Dane named "Blue." My sister, Lori—who was then just a child before she became a member of the teacher's union—was there. We were waiting for the neighbor kids to come out of the house to play. Then Blue attacked, grabbing me by the side of my face, biting and dragging me down the steps. My sister ran down the street screaming bloody murder to get my mom. The neighbor kids' mom came running out of the house, appalled by the scene that now laid on her lap. She picked me up and took me into the house. My face was open, the maul just missing a nerve the plastic surgeon would later say. The ambulance came. Neighbors gathered. The sun simmered and shone. The family was eventually forced to move, else Blue was going to be shot. Less Animal Control than Appalachian Control. It was the first of several traumas involving a head that I'd experience, the chain of events unraveling like a bead of falling dominoes to where I am currently at. In this pirouette with death.

My former psychotherapist once told me about a Vietnam vet that went octopus hunting once a year. He'd take his boat out off the coast of the Atlantic and anchor it. Then he'd jump into depths, sinking from the shallow clarity of the surface world until he found what he was looking for. He'd fight an octopus by hand—"two against six," as my therapist explained it—and then would float to the surface to return to the surface world.

It was not a terribly healthy habit. Dangerous. Inhumane. But the jaunts, the therapist explained, allowed him to leaven his outside with his inside. On the inside, a fondue of memories lived that were always bubbling up if not boiling over. Its substance was the things in war that men do and the sight of the faces and the sound in the voices of those who did, and of those who it was done to. On the outside, a world carried on as if nothing happened. The sun rose. Children played. Politics made faux urgencies legitimate and legitimate urgencies fake. This dissonance...it's enough to make one mad. "I continue to live inside a dichotomy: what was and what shall be," wrote Chila Woychik in *On Being a Rat and Other Observations*. "And the pain in my skull is me trying to mesh the two."[238] Consider the vet's motivation arising from a similar weighted divide, one manifest as a matinee of octopus hunting.

You see, the vet needed the escape of swimming to the edge of near death. It was his drug, that neuronal and nervous system release. In the clinical setting, this is called "repetition compulsion," a term coined by Freud in his 1920 essay "Beyond the Pleasure Principle" to describe the repetitive re-enactment of real events from the past.[239] This is not an isolated phenomenon, mind you, relegated to the realm of the incapacitated and/or diagnosed. The majority of war movies, for example, are scripted with the repetition compulsion as the driving force in the plot. Think Nick's addiction to Russian roulette in *The Deer Hunter*.[240] Or Sgt. James' addiction to defusing bombs in *The Hurt Locker*.[241] Or Colonel Kurtz's addiction to "the horror" in *Apocalypse Now*.[242] The list goes on.

The repetition compulsion also explains how bottomless and commonplace pain is in society, or the predilection for the abused to return to the abuser.[243] Or for the victim to engage in blaming themselves. Then there's inner-city violence. It tends to cluster on specific streets or blocks.[244] It is not spread out anonymously like air but rather bounces back and forth in a cluster of acquaintance from aggressor to victim to future aggressor to future victim as a network effect, just as a contagion, like COVID, moves between more and more people with more and more exposure, ultimately translating into a higher incidence of the negative thing happening. I think of fireworks in a shed. One spark and the booms go off through the proximity of wicks. Except street-level violence restocks itself, with trauma making more trauma through the urge of the traumatized to repeat which, in turn, is fueled by the entropic need to level what's inside with what's out. After all, a hot cup of coffee doesn't stay hot in a cold room. And a cold room doesn't stay cold on a hot afternoon. Consider trauma, then, the hidden playwright of so much of life. A puppeteer of accidents, happenstance, and, in my case, illness. It's a reality perfectly embodied by Freud's analog, the mythicist/psychoanalyst C.G. Jung, who stated: "the psychological rule says that when an inner situation is not made conscious, it happens outside, as fate."[245]

This fate not only echoes within, from, and into the individual, or between individuals, or within and between communities. It can have a long-shadowed effect that crosses time and space, in effect flowing through generations, cultures, and across continents to tie history together, even if that means unraveling history's ingredients: what's current and what's caring. What's happening in Ukraine, for example, will not end when the war ends. What's happening will continue to happen in the memories and motivations of the hurt and unhealed. In his book *My Grandmother's Hands: Racialized Trauma and the Pathway to Mending Our Hearts and Bodies*, the author, Resmaa Menakem, takes aim at the etiology of racial injustice from a psychosocial angle.[246] Menakem's provocation is that racial injustice flows from generations of unprocessed trauma: "White bodies traumatized each other in Europe for centuries before they encountered Black and red bodies. Left unprocessed, that trauma has helped fuel a will to racial supremacy that works emotionally to soothe people whose violent histories made them feel less-than."

Menakem wasn't the first to propose this arguably radical idea that historical trauma that remains unpackaged gets bloomed into norms and behaviors that can be cruel and imposing. In his 1963 bestseller *The Fire Next Time*,[247] the writer James Baldwin perceives what's beyond reproach: Americans don't do well with death. They don't do well with tragedy. "[W]hite Americans do not believe in death," Baldwin goes on in his book-length essay "The Evidence of Things Not Seen,"[248] which covers the context surrounding the Atlanta Child Murders. Baldwin observes that "whoever fears to die also imagines—must imagine—that another can die in his place." "Terror cannot be remembered. Yet, what the memory repudiates controls the human being. What one does not remember dictates who one loves or fails to love." Hence, an external oppression shadow-boxing an internal suppression, all of it unraveling out of our silhouettes to comprise a flow through being in time that fuels our memory of what occurred and our anticipation of what's yet to occur.

And lest we think this psychodrama doesn't have a real-world effect, Baldwin's thesis, for example, helps to explain why working-class whites have been willing to choose racial division over class solidarity, observes the writer James Rowe in the journal *The Arrow*. "Gaining entrée into whiteness is a way of coping with historical trauma."[249]

Hold up, let me make this more plain-spoken, tangible, and digestible for fear of veering off into psychobabble and for making inferences that seem smeared too thin. I am firmly intertwined in the white working class of the inner-city Rust Belt. My lineage, the men at least, tend not to live long. My one grandfather, a veteran of the Winter War between Finland and the Soviet Union—drank himself to death by 50. It was a brutal war, "the Winter War" lost in the annals of WW II. My other grandfather, a Korean war vet and a line worker at the electrical company ("he was always getting shocked," my mom said), died in his mid-50's from esophageal cancer linked to smoking and drinking, as well as continually getting the shit kicked out of him by my grandma's large, Italian brothers (not unreasonably so, from what I am told). My mom's brother, Uncle Rich, a former Teamster and sewage plant worker, recently died of a heart attack in his early 60's, a week before retirement. My dad, Arthur, died at 41. I have brain cancer at 46. A childhood friend, an auto plant engineer, has lost four cousins in the last several years all between the ages of 30 and 50: overdose, homicide, heart failure, and car accident. Every one of us were from—or cut our teeth in—the working-class West Side of Cleveland. No one, outside myself, had a college degree, let alone a graduate degree. And things are not well for that demographic. Or, as Angus Deaton and Anne Case—authors of the book *Deaths of Despair and the Future of Capitalism*[250] [which showed premature deaths have increased four- to five-fold for white, non-college-educated middle-age adults since the 1990s]—put it: "We don't think American capitalism is working for people without a four-year college degree, and that's two-thirds of Americans between the ages of 25 and 64."[251] Simply, workers of all stripes are getting the shaft, and they have been for decades. Why the unbending dissolution of the potentialized force of worker solidarity? Psychologically, I think Menakem and Baldwin are barking up the right tree. Violence, horror, and memory are the ABCs of what Nietzsche called the "eternal return"—a concept framing existence "in terms of endlessly repeating cycles," yet it's an existence embodied "with no transcendent purpose."[252]

Our brains are layered like a red velvet cake, its function and capacity mirroring the evolutionary patterns from which we are ascending. Down below is the reptilian, or instinctual, brain. It is where the alarm bell lives that yells "fight" or "flight." Above that is the limbic system, or mammalian brain, that's involved in our behavioral and emotional responses, especially when it comes to being able to adapt to our environment. It is also where memories live and, thus, where trauma nests. Finally, higher up is the neocortex, which houses rationality and reason, language and imagination. Free will. It's the magic spot where dreams of what could be are made. But it also houses the attic of overthinking it, often ensuring what could be is most certainly not. The issue with trauma is that it's frozen in lower parts of the brain, or still-birthed out of the fight or flight response from which it came to be. And so traditional talk therapy, which works through processes governed by upper parts of the brain, can only do so much to stir the trauma out.[253] Despite years of psycho-therapy, I couldn't escape-valve that which became fossil-ized in my flesh. I couldn't will the sight of seeing my father die out.

I return to Nietzsche's most famous line that "God is dead." The line that follows is less known: "God remains dead. And we have killed him."[254] There has been no lack of ink spilled on what Nietzsche meant. Arguably the most common deciphering flows from the reality that while the era of Enlightenment and Cartesian thought, or the physicalist be-lief that mind is not only separate from matter but is a result of matter, has led to a bounty of innovations and scientia un-der the banner of Aristotelian logic; or things like orbit, math, the COVID vax, our iPhone, Moore's Law and an even better iPhone, this progress also came to prove that there is no scien-tific proof of God's existence. Or as philosopher Bernardo Kastrup recently put it: In man's search for truth we lost the quest for meaning.[255] But this is where we are at. Stuck be-tween the molecular markings of a rock and the spiritual grappling of why there is a "hard place." The evolutionary biologist Richard Dawkins, for instance, writes "scientific beliefs are supported by evidence, and they get results. Myths and faiths are not and do not."[256] Echoes Voltaire: "Faith consists in believing what reason cannot."[257] Such is the tug-of-war of the times.

My god didn't die throughout history, touched off by scratch of a philosopher's pen. My god died in a day. It was June 4th , 1991. I was in the backyard of my father's house. It was a windy, summer day. I had a hockey stick in hand, as I was a hockey player, aged 14. I was hacking at the grass, swinging the stick like a scythe. The day prior, my dad died in a car accident. He was blindsided by a guy running a stop sign. I was in the car too. Unhurt, except for a little cut on my thigh that I got by climbing out from the back window, the black GMC Jimmy resting on its hood after a Dukes of Hazard series of events. I was in the passenger seat and ended up in the back. He was in the driver's seat and ended up in the passenger seat. The symbolism of it all was too much. The stuff of Greek legends. Parents sacrificing for kids and kids trying to redeem that sacrifice in the face of a god-dead sky. The survivor's guilt. The pain. The rapture in the harmony of whatever innocence remains 14 years after birth. It was all beyond words. It often still is. But here we are.

The day of my dad's funeral I went to an amusement park, Cedar Point, with my 8th grade classmates. It was billed as a final outing before high school. Looking back, it was likely inappropriate. I remember walking in, looking at the laughter and kids throwing rings on glass bottles. The smell of cotton candy. The sun was super shiny. Not a hundred steps into the place a crack in my head occurred as it would on a windshield after being hit by pebble that was strewn. The crack ran down the course of my form like a zipper suit. My inside and outside were too far apart. I was stretched too thin. I was cracking in half, a jackknifing sponsored by the two-sided coin of memory and anticipation that became its own Guantanamo Bay in the territory of my body. But for years I didn't know it was there. It was like nothing happened and no one was hurt. But my body kept telling me otherwise.

In August 2021, *The New York Times'* columnist Ezra Klein interviewed psychologist Bessel van der Kolk,[258] author of the best-selling 2014 book about trauma called *The Body Keeps the Score*.[259] Klein had the author on after noticing the book was back up near the top of *The New York Times* bestseller list after a several year hiatus. "That so many of us are turning to [the book during COVID]," he opines, "it says something profound about where the national psyche is in this moment of, yeah, trauma."

"*The Body Keeps the Score* is one of those books people have told me to read for a long time," Klein continued. He admitted to Van der Kolk that because he heard it discussed so many times, he never read it. He believed he knew what it was about, explaining that trauma lodges in the body and is carried as a physical imprint of our psychic wounds and that it's hard to heal. But he acknowledged that once he read it he was wrong about his assumptions. Klein would go on to call the core argument of the book "subversive," explaining that the "devastating argument it makes is not that the body keeps the score, it's that the mind hides the score from us. The mind — it hides and warps these traumatic events and our narratives about them in an effort to protect us."[260]

"Well, trauma is really a wound that happens to your

psyche, to your mind, to your brain," Van der Kolk replied. "Suddenly you're confronted with something that you are faced with horror and helplessness. That nothing prepares you for this and you go like, 'oh, my God'. And so, something switches off at that point in your mind and your brain. And the nature of trauma is that you get stuck there. So instead of remembering something unpleasant, you keep reliving something very unpleasant."[261]

Beyond the repetition compulsion, trauma is also relived through what psychologists refer to as the "soma."[262] Or as the Institut Psychosomatique de Paris explains, "the IPSO works with the theory that trauma is an excessive disorganization in the mental apparatus, and the psychosomatic disease is the alternative that the body finds to discharge excitation, as an attempt to resolve a conflict."[263] Elaborating, while the traumatic experience gets repressed by the mind it doesn't get squished into dissolvable bits. It's instead compacted like a non-biodegradable coil that's all coked up and ready to pop. It gets partitioned in the body like a caged animal whose periodic banging of its confinement is manifested as psychosomatic symptoms, especially the rush of an over-triggered sympathetic and parasympathetic nervous system that floods your blood with the sewage of stress when something, or everything, is perceived as a threat. And the more this happens, the more the barrier of entry is lowered between what's perceived, triggered, and psychosomatically felt. After long, the body becomes the trauma. It keeps the score. Not unlike the city becomes the river it was flooded with. Or the suburban tract houses become the charred remains of the wildfire that blew through via the sloppiness of a charred marshmallow eater. Existence, then, is in many respects but a transfer of energy states. The in blends into the out. The out seeps in. Death becomes life and life becomes death.

By my late 20's, bodily symptoms were commonplace, as was a hypochondriac obsession that every physical symptom, real or not, was a premonition just waiting to be made material. A lot of my symptoms were neurological and or muscular: buzzing in arms and hands. A perceived sense of weakness, etc. This vigilance that something was physically wrong began ramping up by my early 30's. I feared I had MS or a brain tumor. No exaggeration. To compensate, I worked out regularly to prove nothing was physically wrong. I was an avid runner, and the more I physically exerted myself, the more I convinced myself that my body wasn't telling me anything my head didn't already know.

Little did I realize I was in the process of running headlong into the fate I'd convinced myself I was evading. Re: I was being compulsed to repeat. I was eternally returning. It was a drizzly day in July 2007. It was a month or so before my first marriage to Laura, who was the mother of my eldest child. My body was buzzing. I took the bicycle out. It was rush hour. I was trying to cross W. 25th. There were cars coming from both directions and I had to decide to go nor not. I went, going into the middle of the street. Then, a car catty-corner from me was turning left from Franklin Ave. Speeding up. I saw him before he saw me. He was turning into me, going 30 mph plus. I was boxed in by the flow of cross-traffic and so braced myself to go up over the grill. I went up on the hood into the windshield and then into the air, thinking that when I landed I didn't want to die. It was immensely sad. My

life story flashed and unspooled in the theatre of consciousness. When I hit the pavement, I did so with my head. I never
lost consciousness but suffered a traumatic brain injury nonetheless, including a hematoma in my right frontal lobe. I was
taken by ambulance from Franklin Ave. to MetroHealth.
When my dad died he suffered a head trauma on Franklin
Ave., the same street, and was taken not only to MetroHealth,
the same hospital, but also to the trauma center, the same
rooms. You can say fate led me to repeat the trace of his tracks.
A term C.G. Jung called synchronicity, described as "mean-
ingful confidence."[264] And while my survival could've led to a
salvation in a narrative that was being rewritten, it didn't. At
least not then. My trauma wasn't integrated, just compound-
ed. The zone of non-autonomy gaining influence as a black
hole does when its width widens from the eating of galaxies
and stars. Except, here, the hole wasn't so much sucking
things in as spewing things out. Sewage and sewage and sewage. Stress and its effects. The darkening of peach. The mutation of the divine.

Did this confluence of events lead to my glioblastoma?
Rationally, there's a case. From a newer study, the scientist,
Peter Dirks, states: "Our data suggest that the right mutational change in particular cells in the brain could be modified by
[traumatic brain] injury to give rise to a tumour. Glioblastoma
can be thought of as a wound that never stops healing."[265] A
terminal disease caused by a "wound that never stops healing." There's something bottomless about that. Something
evoking the curves of coming full circle. To that end, nothing
happens to us. It happens with us. If not from us. This was
that story.

Mixed Media Print Collage "Love and Geometry"

Worlds Apart:

Midwestern Realism and Transhumanism

When asked about the motive behind the renowned comic book series *American Splendor* that chronicled ordinary people in ordinary Cleveland, its creator, Harvey Pekar, explained, "The theme is about staying alive...Life is a war of attrition. You have to stay active on all fronts...I've tried to control a chaotic universe. And it's a losing battle."[266] After a few bouts with cancer, Pekar would die in 2010 at the age of 70. The cause was complications from prescription medicine.[267]

The aesthetic Pekar dabbled in has been termed "Midwestern realism," a genre described as a way of storytelling that wove in social circumstances with the sentiments of everyday, working-class Americans.[268] A forerunner of this style was Ohio-born William Dean Howells. In a 1917 review of his work in *The Atlantic*, the critics explain that Howells "misses nothing ... of the real, the natural, the colloquial, the moderate, the domestic, and the democratic.[269] William Dean Howells is quite the most American thing we have produced," they continue. "Of the lessons he has taught us, no other seems half so important as the supreme value of having a home, a definitely local habitation, not to tear one's self away from, to sigh for, to idealize through a mist of melancholy and *Weltschmerz*, but simply and solely to live in, to live for."[270]

To live in and live for, I get that. I also get to die from. What I don't get is how one is supposed to do each of these things at once, as is implicitly expected of the incurably and terminally ill who are encouraged to neither be Pollyannaish nor fatalistic about the inevitability of their life's course. How to stay still and keep going? How to fight and acquiesce? Lean in while leaning back? Accept and deny? Perhaps it's a Judo

thing. It's been called the gentlest martial art and is characterized by not opposing the force of the opponent but rather letting that force to be used against its own enforcer.[271]

A few months back, I turned 46. Prior to brain cancer, every birthday was met with a realization that I was getting a
year older, which was kind of depressing as that means you
are one step closer to your life expectancy. Now, I relish it. As
it means I am one step closer to my life expectancy, regardless
of needing a miracle to get there.

Then again, what you expect out of life is infinitely more
significant than meeting the minimum expectations of getting
to die by regressing to the mean. Besides, what does an extra
30 years of me living matter in the yawning unravel that is the
grand scheme of things? I ponder these questions to comfort
me. They don't. But the fact remains that so many souls have
come and gone before us, that number approaching 101 billion dead in the course of human history, according to one
estimate.[272] In fact, the dead outnumber the living by a factor
of 11 to 1.[273] Put another way, there's nothing original about
death. It's only original in that it's your death, and that, by
itself, is unoriginal.

"Thou know'st 'tis common; all that lives must die," ad-
monished Queen Gertrude to her son, Hamlet, in the context
of his moping.[274] Benjamin Franklin made the same point in a
letter to French scientist Jean-Baptiste Leroy, writing, "the
Constitution is now established, and has an appearance that
promises permanency; but in this world nothing can be said
to be certain, except death and taxes."[275]

Yet despite certain certainties, life's grandest mysteries
remain. What happens before and after death? That is the

question. To be or not to be? To be again or not to be again?
The answers aren't clear, unanswerable even. Like trying to
get a good look at the back of your head. But when your death
becomes undeniable and the horizon of your mortality con-
tracts from a distance to the tip of your nose, the Hamlet in us
becomes less literature than the crystal inspiration that com-
pelled Shakespeare to write. When told of her late-stage
breast cancer diagnosis, Alice James, the sister of the famed
psychologist William James and author Henry James who—
upon her posthumously released diaries became famed in her
own right—responded by calling it 'the most supremely in-
teresting moment in life, the only one in fact when living
seems life, and I count in the greatest good fortune to have
these few months so full of interest and instruction in the
knowledge of my approaching death."[276] She'd die at 43.

Meanwhile, "cowards die many times before their
deaths," Shakespeare continues in Julius Caesar. "The valiant
never taste of death but once. Of all the wonders that I yet
have heard. It seems to me most strange that men should fear;
Seeing that death, a necessary end, Will come when it will
come."[277]

Those words are great when hung over the mantel. Or
when birthed into eternity from a legend with his quill. But
take them down and hold them as you are trying to scramble
eggs for your kids, well, this kind of airy insight is about as
useful as an exhale. Useful, no doubt. Vital even. But not exactly in the way a hammer and nail are needed in the process
of hanging something up or holding something down. These
things you can touch. These things you can punch. That's the
stuff of life, right? I mean, try telling your 7- and 10-year old

their dad's incurable cancer and approaching death is just a blessing in disguise. I tried once. The then-7-year-old said, "What is this *death*?" The sound of that response still rattles my cage. The 10-year-old proceeded to draw a self-illustration with a tear in her eye and her hair made of the word "no." "Yes, no," I thought when I saw it, devastated by its brilliance. "She's got it right. Who would say 'yes' to this?"

Sketch with Black Marker, "No"

Source: Angel Piiparinen.

I know. The enlightened. The evolved. The yogis. Ye full
of faith. But I am still just me, bounded by matter and encap-
sulated in an ego. Chockfull of identities. A worker. A dad. A
husband. A Clevelander. A public intellectual. But I am also a
sick person. A terminally ill person. Nearly two years later
and I can still barely drag those last words out of my mouth.
In fact, the longer this goes on the more in denial I get.

There was a book I read just after my diagnosis called
When Breath Becomes Air by Paul Kalanithi. Kalanithi was a
highly-skilled 30-something neurosurgeon who got Stage IV
lung cancer just before he was to end his residency. "I'd suspected I had cancer," he explained in an op-ed in *The New
York Times*.[278] "I had seen a lot of young patients with cancer.
So I wasn't taken aback. In fact, there was a certain relief. The
next steps were clear: Prepare to die. Cry... But on my first
visit with my oncologist," he continued, "she mentioned my
going back to work someday. Wasn't I a ghost? No. But then
how long did I have? Silence."

That op-ed led to a book deal. In his book, he revisits his
initial resignation to being dead already. "It struck me that I
had traversed the five stages of grief — the "Denial • Anger •
Bargaining • Depression • Acceptance" cliché — but I had
done it all backward. On diagnosis, I'd been prepared for
death. I'd even felt good about it. I'd accepted it. I'd been
ready."[279]

I can relate. Upon diagnosis I wrote on Facebook, "So
much of my life has been spent being afraid of dying. With
the time I have left, I endow not to die afraid." I can still hear
the resolute tangibility in my words. As if acceptance of terminal illness is a task that can be met with marching orders or

a deli counter ticket. "If a death was a Bronco," I thought, "I will buck it." Or as the Book of Matthew notes, "May your will be done."[280]

But as Kalanithi's experience continued and he began treatment, he not only found himself going back to work, he became a first-time dad. In both the normalcy and exultancy that followed, a hopeful denial set in. "The rapidity of the cancer science, and the nature of the statistics, meant I might live another twelve months, or another 120," he'd allow…"

The way forward would seem obvious, if only I knew how many months or years I had left. Tell me three months, I'd spend time with family. Tell me one year, I'd write a book. Give me ten years, I'd get back to treating diseases…And now, finally, maybe I had arrived at denial. Maybe total denial. Maybe, in the absence of any certainty, we should just assume that we're going to live a long time. Maybe that's the only way forward."[281]

He'd die at 37.

Neuroscientists have recently been trying to make the case that death denial is less socially- and psychically- constructed than it is an on- and off-switch baked into the "wetware" of the brain. The denial and/or acceptance of death, then, is not so much a matter of transcendental meaning-making but rather a matter of matter, so argue the authors of "Prediction-based neural mechanisms for shielding the self from existential threat."[282] "The brain does not accept that death is related to us," explained a co-author. "We have this primal mechanism that means when the brain gets information that links self to death, something tells us it's not reliable, so we shouldn't believe it."[283]

Scientists such as these can be regarded as materialists, or physicalists.[284] The mental frame these folks take is that mind, or consciousness, is the effect of matter, or brain. The thinking goes that if you squeeze enough synapses and neuronal activity into what cognitive psychologist Daniel Kahneman calls "the meat machine"[285] then conscious awareness—with all its wonder and suffering and loving and longing—comes out the other side of one's sensory inputs, like ground sausage does into its casing. What evidence is there that this is the case? Well, there is none.[286] We just take for granted that our brain "makes" consciousness. If only because our heart pumps blood. And our gut makes gas. "We have made a great deal of progress in understanding brain activity," explains philosopher Philip Goff in *The Conversation*, "and how it contributes to human behavior. But what no one has so far managed to explain is how all of this results in feelings, emotions and experiences. How does the passing around of electrical and chemical signals between neurons result in a feeling of pain or an experience of red?"[287]

Philosopher and computer scientist Bernardo Kastrup, a leader in the emerging field of analytical idealism, takes a different approach. In the *Scientific American* article "Consciousness Goes Deeper Than You Think", Kastrup posits that consciousness may never arise in babies, children or adults, if only because it's always been there to begin with.

> *For all we know, what arises is merely a metacognitive configuration of preexisting consciousness. If so, consciousness may be fundamental in nature...not a property constituted or somehow generated by particular physical arrangements of the brain.*[288]

Simply, what exists "out here" as the "it" or "I" is but an

expression of a universal ground of being that existed "be-fore" us and will exist "after" us.

Famously dubbed the "hard problem of consciousness"[289] by philosopher David Chalmers, it is arguably the hottest in-tellectual debate that you likely never heard of. The only rea-son I began studying it and am bringing it up in this collection is because, truth to be told, I am up against it and am in agi-tated wonder of whether or not my mind will survive in some fashion from my brain's falling apart. Naturally, if there's conscious continuity across life and death then saying good-bye hurts less. This little light of mine has, in fact, led to a roster of reading I wouldn't have otherwise undertaken over the past year and half, including a list of titles that run the gamut from quantum theory to the paranormal to Christian theism to Eastern mysticism and more. There's, for instance, Lipton's *The Biology of Belief,* Schreiber's *Not the Last Goodbye,* Guillen's *Believing is Seeing,* Klean's *Surviving Death,* Schafer's *In Search of a Divine Reality,* Richard Wilhelm's translation of the Taoist text *Secret of the Golden Flower,* and Jung on *Death and Immortality,* with the latter unpacking the mysteries of *The Tibetan Book of the Dead.* "Please guide all beings from this swamp of cyclic existence," wrote the Buddhist mystic Pad-masambhava.[290] I list these titles not to pump myself up as well-read. I don't care. It's only to show how far out of my secular, Westernized comfort zone I'd gone to seek wisdom at best and a lying sense of security at worst. And whether I am trending toward denial or acceptance is in some respects be-yond the point. Goodbye hurts. Comfort is needed, else you just Kafka yourself to death.

I am reminded of an analogy another younger terminally-ill patient said of what her experience was like. She described it as akin to floating in the ocean and slowly being carried out to sea, with the beachgoers on land getting smaller and smaller. The sound of their laughter getting fainter and fainter. It's both terribly sad and wondrously beautiful. It's the tear between the longing to hang onto shore and the relief of the release, all the while knowing you got no choice, besides. Or as the Oak Ridge Boys lyricized, "You don't have to go home but you can't stay here."[291]

"Well, we all die," my oncologist said to me recently while sharing the news of my not-so-good MRI. "You already lived beyond the median life expectancy." My wife was beside me and started to cry. I looked at him sideways, becoming mindful again that physicalists often make below average metaphysicists. But no surprise, MD's are trained to view the world through a tight biological lens. Physical stuff is the cause, like a cellular mutation, and physical stuff is the effect, like a cancer. But in my case, as in the case of many others with rare diseases, there's a hiccup. The effect is nailed down: brain malignancy with certain biomarkers and cell stains that show up reliably in pathology as grade 4 glioma. But the cause is unknown. Which muddies things up more than you'd think. Kind of like watching a game of pool without ever knowing where the cue ball is. The field in front of you is a dizzying array of just effects. Thus, the lack of working treatments. Not to mention the dragging in— as my oncologist did—of musty metaphysical platitudes about expiry, if only as a way to give credence to the notion that everything is under control. There are no mysteries here. The end of the equation is known. Nobody gets out of here alive.

That's our dance, doctors and the incurably ill. It's a ballet described in Atul Gawande's book *Being Mortal* as the struggle to cope with the "constraints of our biology set by genes and cells and flesh and bone" and the power science has to shove against these limits.[292] Gawande, a medical doctor in his own right, acknowledges that such power is finite and always will be.[293] But that fact is increasingly overlooked as the field trends toward the medicalization of mortality, [294] or the process by which the natural and time limited is made into the artificial and time eternal.

If you don't see where this is inevitably heading, this 2021 CNBC Vonnegut-like headline will help, "Silicon Valley's quest to live forever could benefit humanity as a whole."[295] The piece explains that a growing number of tech billionaires, including Amazon's Jeff Bezos, Alphabet's Larry Page, Oracle's Larry Ellison and Palantir Technology's Peter Thiel "have decided they want to use their enormous wealth to try to help humans 'cheat death.'" Cheat death? It is such a heavy-handed, pig-minded Silicon Valley take on what is the most human question there is.

But a take it is. Dubbed transhumanism, it's the ideological belief, notes technology journalist Mark Piesing, "that technology will take us beyond the physical and intellectual limitations of being human," using the likes of nanotechnology, synthetic biology, robotics, AI and digital brain emulation.[296] The end result will be something that appears like immortality, surmises Piesing, who characterizes it as a "posthuman digital entity able to download its consciousness into a synthetic body of choice." It takes the concept of plastic surgery and shotguns it lengthways up the stairway to heaven. It's enough to make the Shakespeare in all of us sick.

Meanwhile, back in Cleveland the issue is far less about cheating death and synthetic bodies than it is figuring out a way to escape the pincers of getting cheated by life and not needing the amputation of limbs: that "shameful metric of inadequate care" as KFF Health News calls it.[297] I see this not-romanticized side of Midwestern Realism every time I am in the outpatient lab in the cancer clinic. The wear and tear on the faces. The wear and tear of the faces. The wheelchairs and walkers. The muffled screams in the eyes of all the onlookers that allow us the stamp of recognition so we can acknowledge each other's presence and thus feel less alone. Many of us are too young to be this old. This waste of potential is a reminder that in my line of work the policy wonks have the audacity to parrot business talking points, like, "Where are the workers?"[298] I want to grab them—one hand by the collar and another by the jowl—and shove them in here and yell, "Here they are!" Now where's the goddamn work?

And then heading even further into the temple of the dog...Back in the exam room. "This is such a shitty disease," I said to the neuro-oncologist as he continued explaining the latest radiological findings. We do this white-knuckled check-up every two months. The anticipatory "scanxiety" (as we cancer survivors call it) is brutal, with one fellow glioblastoma patient analogizing the brain scan process as akin to getting the thumbs up or thumbs down from Caesar. And so there I was: bowed down before the oncologist with the inside of my head imaged on the outside of his computer screen, imagining a giant of antiquity in a leafed crown giving me the yea or nay, with this particular judgement careening toward the latter. My death denial switch was most definitely on *off*.

"This is the end," I thought, the composure I've been fighting to hold together falling apart like a slit bag of jelly. It was only a matter of time now. It was always only a matter of time. "I see by the look on your face where you are going with this," the oncologist said. "There's no need. You've only completed your first line of therapy. You're healthy and strong". His assurances didn't stop the cascade of woes coming from our side of the aisle. "I am here for you both," he'd say. "Thanks," I replied, "I know."

I did. My doctor was a solid, guy. A Rust Belter from Toledo. A shopkeeper whose shop was shredded by the grooves of the machine's wheels. After he left my wife and I curled up in a ball of spittle and tears, waiting for the nurse to come in to schedule another scan so we can do this all over again in a month or so, if not sooner. Undeniably sooner. A bad scan only leads to more scans more frequently. More scanxiety. Likely more surgery. I already got the Gigli saw. There's talk this time of the drill and the blow torch. In the brain. Bah. (Author's note: The less invasive drill/torch surgery got denied by insurance, Medical Mutual. The Gigli saw it was. Insurers can be so garish and gory. I couldn't imagine living forever like this. I'd take the shot at nothingness versus everything over the guaranteed download of an awareness that is getting machined over. There's a name for that: "purgatory." And there's nothing human, let alone transhumanistic, about it.

We gathered ourselves, got up. And headed out. It's summer in Cleveland. Life is all full bloom. The previous winter had pounded the city—the biting wind landing in the bones of us, and the piles of dirty snow creating mini mountains on the sidewalks that made it harder to move forward when it was already hard enough. Now it's the ecology of a city and its humidity. Cicadas burping everywhere, bumping up against the sound of crickets, church bells, ambulances, and freight trains. That Rust Belt symphony, the ambient sound of home. It's a home to live in. To live for. To fight for. And, yes, to sink with.

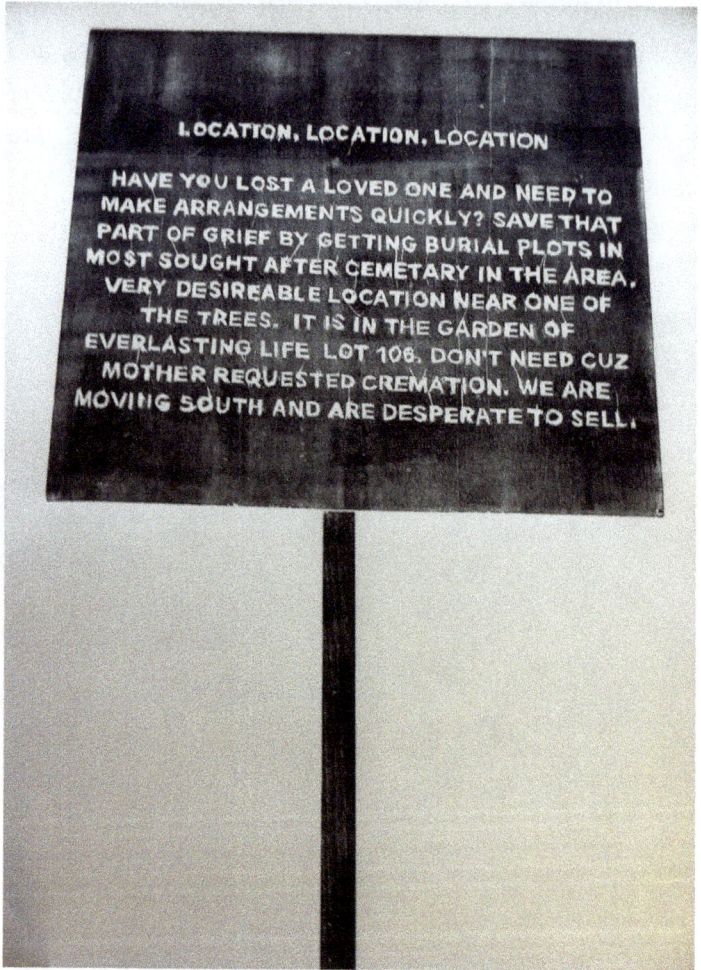

Illustration, "Location, Location, Cremation".

Mesofacts,
Man Boobs,
and
Managed
Decline

Statistical mathematician and author of the book *The Black Swan: The Impact of the Highly Improbable,* Nassim Taleb, had this to say about the social scientist's ability to predict future events. "We know from chaos theory that even if you had a perfect model of the world, you'd need infinite precision in order to predict future events. With sociopolitical or economic phenomena, we don't have anything like that."[299] The Chinese philosopher Lao Tzu made a similar point in a different way, "Those who have knowledge, don't predict. Those who predict, don't have knowledge."[300]

Yet that doesn't stop people from grabbing the mic and making a go of it. In a 2016 *Atlantic* piece contentiously entitled "Do Parts of the Rust Belt 'Need to Die Off'?",[301] Galen Newman, a landscape architecture and urban planning professor from Texas A&M, was interviewed by Alexia Fernández Campbell, a journalist from Florida. While each of their Rust Belt bona fides are questionable in terms of weighing in on such a localized, if heavy, topic, it didn't stop them from having takes. And then publishing them in a national magazine for the rest of the world to be informed by.

Right out of the gate, Campbell posed a question that had Newman rubbing and gazing into his crystal ball. "How do you envision the future of the Rust Belt?" "What I think is going to happen is that a lot of these old, large cities are going to die out," he'd say, borrowing from the terminology of a paleontologist, absent the metaphorical layup of swapping out the city of Buffalo for the extinct species known as Bison antiquus. Campbell then changed his tone toward that of a hospice nurse before landing in the breadbasket of a pro-death prosecutor. "I don't think they're going to officially die, but I think we're going to have to **let some of them go**. We need to accept that some of these big **cities need to die**, pieces of the **city need to die off**..."[302]

It's a tough and borderline unconscionable take, yet one vacuum-packed in the cushion of subject matter expertise. Newman went on to explain that he was consulting with a number of Rust Belt cities, advising them on a strategy that'd become known as "smart" or "managed" decline. Consider it palliative care for cities. He mentioned "a tool" he developed that was able to predict what neighborhoods are candidates for the wrecking ball. You got to have a steel stomach to play in this mud, i.e., the demolishing of homes at scale. And it left such a bad taste in my mouth that I penned a counter to the Campbell/Newman piece in *The Atlantic's City Lab* called "Smart Decline is Dumb."[303] The subheading read, "We don't know the future. Rust Belt cities need to stop planning that there isn't one." The takeaway of the piece was this: if your city's plan is to manage decline then you are going to get, well, decline. Cleveland's newly-elected Mayor, Justin Bibb, seemed to get that message, writing in his 2022 Rescue and Transformation Plan that "we're moving away from managing decline to making investments that drive growth in Cleveland's neighborhoods that have been overlooked or excluded in the past."[304]

Now whether that strategy is executed appropriately is another thing, but at least it's a view of the world that doesn't chain yourself to the letdowns of yesterday, creating for an infinity of indigestion in the built form and, in turn, the lived experience and, in turn, the inclination to rebuild, burn, or bulldoze. And not just on the outside of yourself. But on the inside of yourself as well. "I cannot make anyone understand what is happening inside me," wrote Franz Kafka in *Metamorphosis*, "I cannot even explain it to myself."[305]

Still, why did Newman make the argument he did? To take such a hardline stance you've got to have good reason, right? Newman's predictions that parts of the Rust Belt "need to die" were based on historic population trends. The Rust Belt loses people and the Sun Belt gains people. And given there's more job growth in the Sun Belt than the Rust Belt the trends weren't about to change any time soon. A version of the same point has been made from all angles all of the time to the point that none of it means anything. When everyone is parroting talking points, that's not useful knowledge. That's consensus that paves the way for path dependencies. Missing from Newman's crystal ball world, however, were the suddenly impactful "black swan" events, like COVID, that's given rise to the era of telecommuting and has decoupled the need to live near where you work. You don't have to reside in San Francisco, for example, to be employed at Facebook or Google. You can live on the shores of Lake Erie, which could indeed be viewed more favorably as the flooded- and sun-parched patches of earth get additionally flooded and sun parched.[306]

Also missing from Newman's prognostications were the slower-moving, structural happenings, such as crashing global fertility rates that's affected immigration as a viable source of growth for America's gateway cities. According to the latest demographic projections from the UN, the world's population is set to peak at about 10.9 billion in 2100.[307] The annual growth rate of the world population has already peaked, going from 2.1% in 1968 to 1.1% in 2019. By 2100, the UN projects the annual growth rate to hit nadir at 0.1%. "Just as expected by demographers," explains Max Roser, "the world as a whole is experiencing the closing of a massive demographic transition."[308]

So what? Well, what it means is that less people are available to more cities facing stagnating growth. Something's gotta give. And when it does (as it is) what was historically continuous can quickly become discontinuous wherein the past is no longer effectively precedent. As the emergent trends above age into existence an argument can, in fact, be made that the Rust Belt has fallen less behind America's "undying" parts, if only because those parts are catching up to "being Rust Belt." Which has had me wondering. Is Cleveland a failure or a forewarning? Is it a canary in the coal mine or just another roadside vulture that's mocked?

The latest Census population estimates showed that nearly 75% of U.S. counties had more deaths than births from 2020 to 2021.[309] Never before in the nation's history has there been a higher concentration of places experiencing a natural decrease in population.[310] In academic parlance, this is what is called "demographic decline." What's more, the population loss that's become commonplace in the Rust Belt has spread like a disease into various jeweled cities of the U.S. The map below shows the top 20 counties nationally with the largest decreases in population from 2020 to 2021. No Rust Belt county, outside of Detroit's Wayne, makes the list. The places that lost the most population compile a who's who of coastal counties. Some of the major cities whose county seats experienced the largest population declines include:

Chicago, Los Angeles, Manhattan, Brooklyn, San Francisco, Seattle, Washington, D.C., Miami, Dallas, and Boston.

Top 20 Counties Largest Population Losses, 2020-2021. lation Estimates.

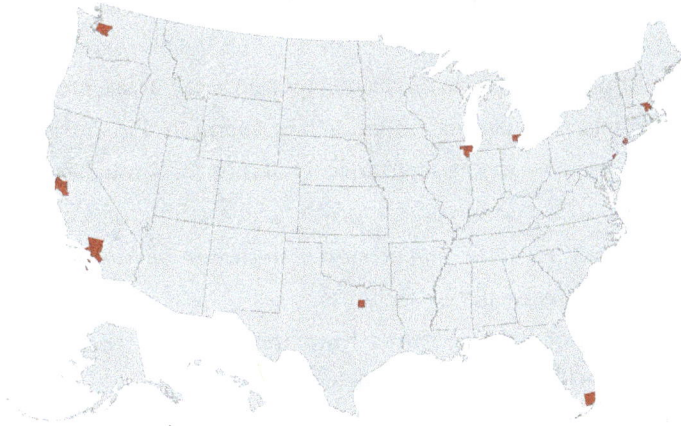

Of course, no one would ever consider these places as dying and in need of being "let go." That's just not the way we think of coastal cities. While it's the only way we think of the Rust Belt. "As if one believed anything by instinct! One believes things because one has been conditioned to believe them," writes Aldous Huxley in *Brave New World*.[311] At some point, though, the chains of past perception get broke, letting out the breath of fresh eyes. Inevitably, everything gets tired and falls part. Even the posture of so-called "superstar cities."[312] That's not a prediction. That's a mesofact.

In *The Boston Globe* op-ed "Warning: Your reality is out of date," Samuel Arbesman breaks down the components of knowledge by the type of facts we get informed by.[313] There are facts that don't change, like the capital of Finland is Helsinki. And there are fast-changing facts, like the value of the

NASDAQ on a day-to-day basis. In between are mesofacts, or facts that are neither fast- nor no-changing but no less game-changing, as long as they aren't disallowed from being realized. "[I] imagine you are considering relocating to another city," writes Arbesman. "Not recognizing the slow change in the economic fortunes of various metropolitan areas, you immediately dismiss certain cities. For example, Pittsburgh, a city in the core of the historic Rust Belt of the United States, was for a long time considered to be something of a city to avoid. But recently, its economic fortunes have changed, swapping steel mills for technology..."

He's not lying. Figures from the Bureau of Economic Analysis (BEA) charting real per capita personal income[314] show that among the nation's largest, powerhouse 40 metro areas, Pittsburgh's per capita income of ($59,975) ranks 13th. Milwaukee ($59,752) is 14th . The Cleveland metro ($57,094) is 21st. These aren't the vitals of the dead. Why the last rites?

Daniel Kahneman is a Nobel laureate famous for his research into how biases lead us to make irrational decisions when all we really want is to make the best decision. Speaking at a conference on artificial intelligence, Kahneman explained, "We have in our heads a wonderful computer. It's made of meat, but it's a computer. It's extremely noisy — it does parallel processing, it is extraordinarily efficient – but there is no magic there." Kahneman's point was that people are not really good at evaluation and decision-making. And it's not just biases clouding our judgment, he explains, but also the noise from our overloaded senses that clogs our information processing systems, rendering us less than. Kahneman makes the case that AI algorithms "should replace humans whenever possible."[315] The AI he is referring to, here, is not the transhumanistic singularity gobbledygook in which computer scientists figured out how to reverse engineer god. But rather using technology to supplement human constraints in cognition as it pertains to the ability to focus, evaluate, and increase the probability of interventional success. This is not unlike how we use pistons and pumps to supplement the limitations in the human body related to strength, speed, precision, and stamina, all the while getting the job we wanted done, done.

Enter man boobs. In 2006 the NBA's Houston Rockets hired Daryl Morey to be their GM. The intent was to bring sabermetrics from baseball to basketball, or to algorithmically systematize the likelihood of a given player's success. To do this, Morey developed a basic algorithm. In 2007 his model really liked European prospect Marc Gasol, who eventually became a multi-year All-Star. But they passed on him and so did every other team. Why? "The scouts had found a photograph of him shirtless," Michael Lewis writes in his book about behavioral economics and the science of decision making, *The Undoing Project*.[316] "He was pudgy and baby-faced and had these jiggly pecs. The Rockets staff had given Marc Gasol a nickname: Man Boobs." Simply, Gasol didn't "look" like what a successful NBA player is supposed to be. The image stuck in their heads, then, was acting as noise and clouding clear judgment. Gasol was summarily derided and dismissed. In fields of all stripes, people, including subject matter experts, are bad at judging and predicting success. That's because individuals use heuristics, or mental shortcuts, when making decisions, which often do more harm than good. The heuristic employed in the man boob's case was "representativeness", wherein the chance of success was made by comparing what something looks like (Marc Gasol) against what we think it should look like (LeBron James). The corollary, here, is that Rust Belt cities (Cleveland) don't look like what successful cities look like (San Francisco). Importantly, it's not the perception of non-success that is the only problem. Rather, it's the fix that gets offered that ends up making things worse.

In the study "Demolition As Urban Policy in the American Rust Belt," planning professor Jason Hackworth of the University of Toronto found that "there are 269 neighborhoods in 49 cities that have lost more than 50 percent of their housing since 1970."[317] This wave of destruction has claimed more homes than urban renewal efforts, or that wholesale destruction of communities by the federal government in the first half of the 20th century for, among other things, the inlaying of highways. But Hackworth found these demolitions have "not led to market rebound or a decrease in social marginality." Instead, those Rust Belt neighborhoods with the most disassembly since 1970 didn't get better, they got worse. Echoing this conclusion, Alan Mallach—a scholar on legacy cities who'd been "bullish on demolition"—told *The Washington Post* that "demolishing a lot of houses might be removing that neighborhood's chance to revive in the future."[318] This is not to say demolition isn't a necessary tactic when used as part of larger redevelopment framework. The problem arises when a stand-alone policy of demolition is regarded as a path to rebirth.

"This article argues that the human body should be considered as a geographical object," so reads the first line of an essay by French geographer, Guy Di Méo, in the journal *Annales de Géographie*.[319] Though unmade of rocks and rivers, the human body nonetheless impacts and is impacted by what's going on in the geographies around them. You can also take Di Méo's statement and invert it, losing none of its poetry and reflection. It would read thusly: "This article argues that the geographical city should be considered as a human body." This is, in fact, how city builders and planners have historically conceived of their "canvas." Not so much as made of bricks and wood as of bones and flesh. A 1951 *Chicago Tribune* piece, for example, refers to one urban renewal project as a "slum facial" under the title "Big South Side Area is Getting Her Face Lifted."[320]

Close your eyes for a moment and think of what a Rust Belt city looks like. What do you see? The aesthetics of ruin, abandonment, and decay. Concentrated poverty. City blocks homogenized by skin color. Skeleton factories. Houses with hollow eyes for windows, and houses so overgrown with earth that the nature unbridled is tearing the domicile from the inside out. Things broken. Things slanted. Bits and pieces relieved of their function and forms to lay loosely in piles, if not fully decomposed into absence. If the Rust Belt city was a body, then, it would be disfigured. The scars would be a blight, defined as "a thing that spoils or damages something,"[321] with the "something" in this case being the aesthetic quality of place. And while blight is often a local effect to global causes— i.e., socioeconomic distress flowing downstream into communities from macro forces such as deindustrialization—it can also be self-inflicted, wherein the ugly is manufactured through the unbending thirst for beauty.

Disfiguration, in a sense, is but an endpoint along the path of cosmetic want. There's a medical condition called scab picking, or excoriation, that comes to mind. After some kind of rash, skin infection, or small injury, a person may pick at the scab, which causes more injury to the skin and keeps the lesion from healing. Done long enough, scab picking can turn into an obsessive-compulsive psychological condition called "dermatillomania"[322] that leads to infection and permanent scarring. The viscerality of the scab picker is not unlike the viscerality of the demolisher. In both cases there's an urge beyond language and logic to excavate the root of a bad happening.

The field of city building has a long and sordid history of trying to make the ugly beautiful. Or to bring its atrophying parts back to life. There are numerous points of entry here. I choose to lead with investigative journalist Jacob Riis' classic *How the Other Half Lives* published in 1890.[323] It's standard reading for every city builder in training. The book—part literary exposé, part photographic documentary—was essentially a slum tour of Manhattan meant as a wake-up call for elites. And though a main aim was to help usher in the Progressive Movement with the creation of tenement houses, soup kitchens, child labor laws and the like, Riis' interpretation as to what caused the slum had a secondary, equally long-shadowed, impact. A close confidant of Theodore Roosevelt, Riis began insisting on the importance of the aesthetic environment in slum creation. Or as Riis argued in an article he wrote for the *New-York Tribune*, "it is not the squalid people that make the squalid houses, but the squalid houses that make the squalid people."[324] The solution? To make what's dirty clean.

So arose the architecture and urban design era termed "The City Beautiful Movement."[325] At its core it was a crusade to prettify cities. The purpose was two-fold. Leaders wanted to keep the elites in the city, so they created swaths of frontier-like park space to eliminate the urge to flee. Second, prettify-ing was seen as a reformative way to fix the disagreeable in the masses. Think beauty as social control. "When they trum-peted the ameliorative power of beauty," wrote the scholar Paul Boyer in the essay "The Ideology of the Civic Arts Move-ment in America, 1890-1910," "they were stating their belief in its capacity to shape human thought and behavior."[326] Sim-ply, an outside order meant an inside order, with a growing collection of inside orders flowing out into the stepwise knit-ting of a harmony within society. If the City Beautiful Move-ment was executed properly, the thinking went, the promise of the metropolis would be perpetually stilled, reflecting like a Matisse. Reads the opening of the 1904 treatise *Modern Civic Art*; or, The City Made Beautiful:

There is a promise in the sky of a new day. The darkness rolls away, and the buildings that had been shadows stand forth dis-tinctly in the gray air. The tall facades glow as the sun rises; their windows shine as topaz; their pennants of steam, tugging flutteringly from high chimneys, are changed to silvery plumes. Whatever was dingy, coarse, and ugly, is either transformed or hidden in shadow. The streets, bathed in the fresh morning light, fairly sparkle, their pavements from upper windows ap-pearing smooth and clean. There seems to be a new city for the work of the new day.[327]

But there was a problem with this approach. Namely, an outside order does not create an inside order. The feedback between the out and the in just like the feedback between an inhale and an exhale. Inseparable. That said, fixing what's broken on the inside of the only agent of change there is: the individual, is yeomen's work. The manufacturing of human well-being is a marathon not a sprint. What's easier is pointing to the vacant house and saying, "There it is, go and burn it." And then pointing to the burnt-out house and saying, "There it is, bulldoze it." Perhaps predictably, think of blight as the malignance on the body of a city. It's easier to treat cancer by beating the body into submission, hoping the tumor dies before you do. It's harder to engender wellness by rejoining all of what's connected that's been pulled apart: land to body, body to mind. Mind to soul, soul to spirit. The gist is that the sick cannot just heal from the outside in via ingestion or incision. The infirm also must heal from the inside out. But it's just not how things are done. Or will be done.

I recently came across a talk by the philosopher Alan Watts called "The Myth of Myself."[328] A few lines are resonant. "[We] speak of coming into this world," Watts would say about halfway through, "and this whole sensation that we are brought up to have of being an island of consciousness locked up in a bag of skin, facing outside us, a world that is profoundly alien to us in the sense that what is outside 'me' is not me, this sets up a fundamental sensation of hostility and estrangement between ourselves and the so-called external world." It's an estrangement, I'd argue, that leads to humanity's incessancy to dominate space and waste time. The city is a breeding ground for this unfolding. It's where many of these battle lines are drawn and fought.

It was an autumn day in Cleveland, 1965. Cleveland Mayor Ralph Locher had just officiated the city's first "home burning ceremony." It was a new tactic of blight remediation. Locher was convinced that a "controlled burn" strategy would reduce the costs of demolishing vacant homes and help spark a resurgence of Cleveland's real estate market, which was then beginning to founder as manufacturing jobs fled the city.

The first of four houses that burned did so in an hour, "aided by a stiff breeze and 20 gallons of kerosene," the *Cleveland Press* reported.[329] "I'd never thought I'd stand by and watch a place burn," the mayor marveled, "but this is a beautiful sight, isn't it? It has such a cleansing effect." Locher's burns were but part of a larger firestorm that engulfed Cleveland, so documents Daniel Kerr in his 2012 analysis "Who burned Cleveland, Ohio? The forgotten fires of the 1970s."[330] By one measure, population growth, you could argue Locher's policy efforts had an impact. Between 1970 and 1980, the city would experience the steepest population loss in its history, an attrition of every 1 out of 4 residents.[331] You might say that Cleveland managed to manage decline impeccably. Beautifully even.

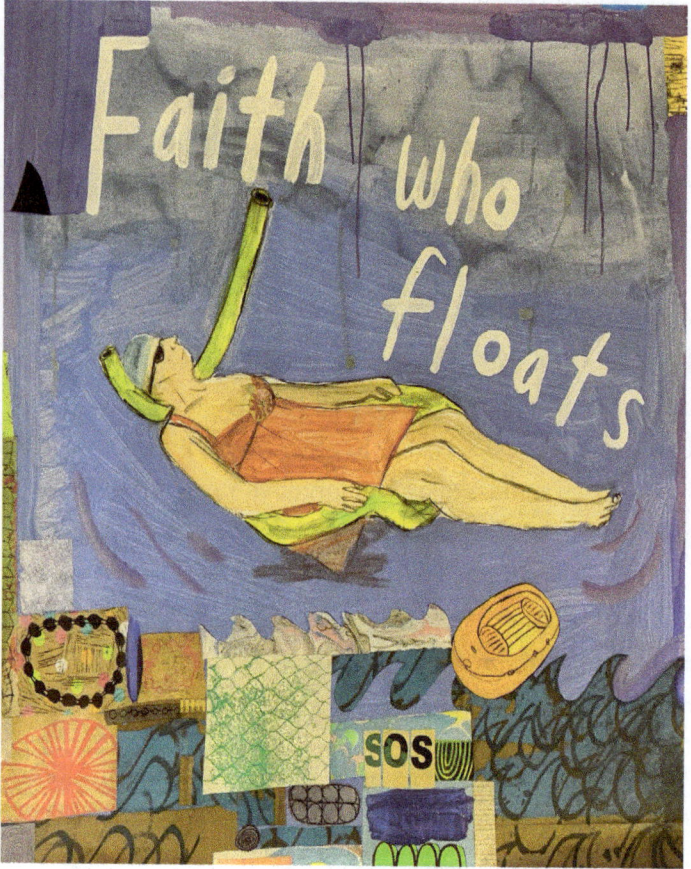

Mixed Media Print Collage Rough Waters, for Faith,

What's the Matter with Matter:

Apostles Versus Geniuses and a Guillotine Necklace

Every 9 A.M. the church bells of St. Jerome ring outside my window, the cling clang positioning for a sound that seems to amplify and crest with each toll before dissolving into the other sounds of Cleveland's broken daybreak. On this particular morning what emerged from the church bell's calming was the noise of backyard dogs barking. And, of course, there's the constant buzz of cicadas, all of them living their loud lives somewhere. In the grass, the bushes, and the trees.

My cancer has recurred. The anti-being is back to being its sick self. Growing on its host in the kamikazed act of killing us both. I was diagnosed with what's considered a terminal illness, glioblastoma multiforme (GBM), nearly two years ago. I read somewhere that a terminal illness meant a person had six months, more or less. That seemed reasonable. But what does the mind do with the notion that they're wearing a guillotine necklace for 2, 3, 4 years out? I'm not sure there is an answer other than to live and let live and then die and find out.

Not infrequently I succumb to the thought pattern that a sense of security can be found, just as long as you keep feverishly looking. Security snuggles up to the known, whereas insecurity gets mined from what's unknown. Enter the general-purpose technology known as "the internet," defined as "a global communications network...typically interconnected by fiber optic cabling...that is at once a world-wide broadcasting capability, a mechanism for information dissemination, and a medium for collaboration and interaction between individuals and their computers without regard for geographic location."[332] It's also arguably the greatest innovation in the history of mankind in the effort to make the unknown

known. Though existentially naive, I sometimes try to get information on what happens after death the same way I try to find out what's playing at the local theatre. I Google it. Whether that'll lead to any semblance of wisdom or transcendental enlightenment is highly unlikely. But that's no matter. Googling by now has become a human gag reflex, done when feeling ornery and anxious. Insecure. Which is everyone, everywhere, all the time. Moreover, the response of the Magic 8 Ball hive mind that is the algorithmic query search engine is—while imperfect—still telling, since it gives you the page-ranked answers to everybody's question. If you search, for instance, for "what happens after life" from a Cleveland IP address, the top three hits you get are Wikipedia's "Afterlife" page. An article from the Church of Jesus Christ of Latter-day Saints' website entitled "What happens after we die." And a Cleveland Clinic piece, "What happens when you die."

Wikipedia gets to the heart of the matter quickly, referring to an "afterlife" as "a purported existence in which the essential part of an individual's identity or their stream of consciousness continues to live after the death of their physical body."[333] This continuity of consciousness, Wikipedia continues, may be a partial element, or a person's entire soul or spirit. "Belief in an afterlife is in contrast to the belief in oblivion after death," the article concludes. You could say Wikipedia is pretty agnostic in its presentation of information on what happens after death, as it frames the either/or of afterlife versus oblivion as being precursored by "belief." That is, the question of what's after life is thrown back onto the subjectivity of the reader, which is not surprising given Wikipedia is a secular, crowd-funded information repository dealing with "just the facts, Jack." But there's no answer there. It's still just you and your worries and hopes, either looking upward and praying or monitoring the geometry of terrestrial bodies. It's Galileo or Godot.

This is in contrast to distinct metaphysical or theological positions taken up by entities with more skin in the game. Take the Church of Jesus Christ of Latter-day Saints' article mentioned previously. It is far less unequivocal in answering questions about the afterlife, explaining that: "When we die our spirit and body are detached. The spirit is the essence of the 'I' and goes to the spirit world."

The spirit world is a waiting period until we receive the gift of resurrection, when our spirits will reunite with our bodies. Our future resurrected body cannot die and will be perfect—free from pain, sickness, and imperfections. It is because of the infinite love of Jesus Christ that everyone will be resurrected.[334]

The Cleveland Clinic query hit doesn't broach the prospect of an afterlife, answering only the question, "What happens to your body when you die? The shift back to the body makes it a question solely about expiry, with transcendent meaning shoved out of sight. Life is a television with reception experienced as perception. What happens when you unplug the cord? The Clinic piece answers:

Death marks that moment in life when your physical body stops working to survive. You breathe your last breath. Your heart stops beating. Your brain stops. Other vital organs, including your kidneys and liver, stop. All your body systems powered by these organs shut down, too, so that they're no longer capable of carrying on the ongoing processes understood as, simply, living."[335]

In other words, pay no mind to mind, all that matters is matter. And the former is caused by the latter.

This ideological stance is called "metaphysical materialism."[336] It suggests that the existence of matter is independent of mind. Not only that, through evolutionary processes kicked off by theoretical events such as "the Big Bang," matter gives rise to mind. Our lives and our relations and our crimes and commitments are nothing but an aggregating upward of glossary terms you'd find in high school curriculum text conceived circa the 18th and 19th century. The problem, though, is that this "theory of everything" has never come close to being proven. There's no viable conceptual or theoretical model of how it happens, let alone an empirical validation proving causality that matter mind.

What's more, critics of this view, such as philosopher Bernardo Kastrup, the author of *Why Materialism is Baloney*[337] and founder of the Essentia Foundation, are becoming increasingly vocal, if only because both the logic and empirical proof behind the materialist ideology—when looked at judiciously—just doesn't pass muster. This has coincided with a growing chorus of critics that have come to refer to the fervent belief in materialism as "the dogma of science,"[338] which inevitably pokes its head up when the unexplainable occurs. And this is often.

In a 2021 *Scientific American* article entitled "When Scientific Orthodoxy Resembles Religious Dogma,"[339] the writer, astronomer Avi Loeb, who is the author of the book *Extraterrestrial*, explained the pushback he received by fellow astronomers when he suggested that the first interstellar object detected in our solar system, Oumuamua, might have been made by another civilization. "Innovation blossoms in a culture willing to acquire new knowledge rather than being trapped in its past belief system," Loeb writes."[340] "A mainstream astronomer who worked on rocks in the solar system for decades commented grudgingly: 'Oumuamua is so strange.... I wish it never existed.'"[341]

Such is an exemplar of the security of the known. Consider it a modern-day "opiate of the masses"[342] —that term economist Karl Marx used for culture's spiritual search for belonging that revved up during the rise of The Enlightenment and the attendant Industrial Revolution. But instead of finding comfort in the divine, modern society commonly reaches out toward the promise of technological progress. In this respect, Steve Jobs was Job. "You clothed me with skin and flesh, and knit me together with bones and sinews,"[343] said Job to God. "Innovation distinguishes between being a leader and a follower," said Jobs to his followers, or what Benjamin Zeller at The University of Chicago Divinity School referred to as "the cult of Apple."[344]

I am aware I am treading into an unsafe space—or that conflict in veracity between religion and science. And while this conflict has rearisen in the age of COVID and the anti-vax, it is a conflict that is neither new, nor particularly valid, so argues the Danish philosopher Søren Kierkegaard, who wrote in his book *The Present Age and of the Difference Between a Genius and an Apostle*: "A genius and an Apostle are qualitatively different, they are definitions which each belong in their own spheres: the sphere of immanence, and the sphere of transcendence."[345]

I was raised Roman Catholic, attending St. Ignatius Elementary on West Boulevard in Cleveland's Near West Side until 6th grade, then St, Edward High School on the Lake-wood/Cleveland border. I call this "city Catholic," or being part of a Catholic culture but no so much part of a religious community. It's basically a have-your-cake-and-it-too ap-proach to spirituality, doing what you want to do as it served you. Don't eat meat on Friday. Go to mass on Sunday. Drink to get pig drunk the rest of the week. While I know religion, I am not religious per se. Yes, I know this is a cop out. Ye have faith or not? I think I do. I do, I think.

Still, I am just trying to survive, doing what science tells the doctors to do when there's evidentiary reason to do so, but also taking an integrative oncological approach if there is no there there from a treatment standpoint, but there is a "there there" from a standpoint of need. I see an integrative oncologist who specializes in reiki, a holistic practitioner who advises me on herbal supplements and diet, and a Sha-man who specializes in whole-person healing. And yes, I am back to saying the "Our Father" and "Hail Mary" every night. I try to find an inner connection between my mind and body via the divine that I lost. This reminds me of the first time I talked to the shaman—a man who had a Near Death Experience (NDE)[346] and met dozens of his incarnates—I said I didn't so much "need to be cured as healed." From then on out we were on the same page. Perhaps amusingly, I do Zoom sessions with the energy healer, sessions I refer to as "Zoomin'" with my shaman." I see him not only as a spiri-tual guide (he was trained in various indigenous traditions), but he also turned out to be one of the most insight-inducing therapists I ever had. I asked him once why he didn't he go down the traditional healing route? As in counseling. "I find it…" he began…" "Devoid of spirit," I cut in. "Yes, "said the Shaman, who is Caribbean-born, Peruvian-trained, and Sun Belt-based.

Life is a goddamn trip. From where I started to where I went through to where I am now. For those traditionalists who say, "Why? Let science handle it." I do. I have. More often than not, though, the empiricists themselves lead the path forward back to faith. I have, for instance, have had dozens of conversations with top-notch cancer specialists, and so many had shades of the one below. Take 'em for what they are worth. I am not here to convince anyone of anything, be it in the land of imminence or transcendence. I call it like I see it and just want to breathe. I just want to be able to breathe with my family and watch my kids grow up. Just like you. You are not unlike me. We're the same in many of our unalike ways.

Me: How much time do I got?
Doctor: Not sure, everyone is different.
Me: But there are people who live with glioblastoma for many years?
Doctor: Yes, but they are rare.
Me: Do we know why they survived as long as they did?
*Doctor: *Shoulder shrug* No. But what I can say is, think positively and aim high.*
Me: Okay.

Probabilistically, I had a decent run. This isn't to say you can put a fork in me. You'd never know I was sick. There's nothing yet on the outside that reflects my contrast enhancement, absent my craniotomy scar that slays and marks me as

arguably intriguingly discordant, both vulnerable and vener-
able. As of this writing, I still work out every day and work
full time. I write. So to say I had a decent run is only to say
that I'm entering into a next phase of my illness—one technically called "second-line therapy," defined by the NIH as
"treatment that is given when initial treatment (first-line therapy) doesn't work or stops working."[347] And while there can
be upwards of 6 or 7 lines of treatment for my illness, the
more that's done to your body to keep you alive, then the
more that's done to your body to keep you alive. Eventually
there comes a point of diminishing returns. When that will be
I don't know nor do my doctors. But with cancer of the brain,
that line is comparably not hard to reach. The brain, after all,
is the point of contact for treatment. The brain is also the point
of contact for the momentary state of experience that flows
into the more enduring state of existence. The more, then, that
my wetware gets burnt, poisoned, and cut, the more my issues become a feature and not a bug. We are playing a zero-
sum game in many respects. Just as there is no such thing as
blowing a candle lit.

Regardless, my treatment is happening as the healthcare
industry was designed to proceed. You got cancer? Enter
here. Services are rendered and receipts are then stacked on
the cashier's spike, until the leaning tower of chemo falls over
on the backs of the people who ultimately become the pur-
chasers of their own prototype. Like going to the deli to buy
our own pound of flesh. The figure below shows just how
much the American economy is becoming dependent on con-
suming its own well-being. In 1970, 6.2% of the U.S. Gross
Domestic Product (GDP) was spent on healthcare expendi-

tures, rising to nearly 19% by 2020. By comparison, other G7 nations range from 9.6% of national GDP spent on healthcare expenditures in Italy to 12.9% in Canada.[348] This is not a viable path forward. No matter how hard you squint, the plasma bank will never be the *bank* bank. Sickness will never produce development. Profit, yes. Disease and yield are the peanut butter and jelly of social ills. But only health is wealth. Sickness is sickness. Don't overthink what's grimacing and staring you plain in the face.

Percent of U.S. GDP on Healthcare Expenditures, 1970 to 2020.

Source: OECD

If my cancer recurrence sounds unideal that's because it is. There's no sugarcoating that, and I am not about to try. The median life expectancy for those with recurrent glioblastoma is…well, I don't even want to go there. I'd rather put things into perspective. Two metrics, here, are illustrative. There's a term healthcare practitioners and researchers use called "overall survival" (OS). It charts how far you made it from diagnosis until death. For glioblastoma multiforme the median OS is about 14 months. Another important metric is progression free survival (PFS).[349] Glioblastoma has a near 100% chance of recurring after completion of first-line therapy, i.e., standard of care. In fact, remission is not really a term used in malignant, high-grade glioma, although there exist legendary exceptions, such as Ben Williams, author of *Surviving "Terminal" Cancer*,[350] who would ultimately just die of death. The median time to recurrence, or PFS, be it a new tumor growing or a residual tumor progressing, is about 8 to 10 months. They found my tumor radiologically Jan. 5th 2021. As I write this, it's September 8th , 2022. I've made it 20 months without recurrence. Almost at the two-year mark. That's good. I mean, none of this is good, but we're painting with shades of gray here.

Besides, it's not the time for fear. Fear is a snake that slithers into your DM's. It's a dead emotion on a dead moon. And I've got to pack lightly. I can't afford to carry regrets over into the land I always imagined existed but have a hard time having faith in. All the while, the living is all around me. The church bells ring. The dogs bark. The raindrops drop. My wife worries wordlessly. By mom worries busily. My kids worry puzzlingly. I cry, I cry, I cry. Blending in the colors out of their Machiavellian imposition. I feel the clock ticking, and I want to take the hands of time and handcuff them to the anchor of eternity. I want to gather the troops and tell them there's nothing to worry about. I want to gather the troops and tell them this is not the end. I want to gather the troops and tell them that even the end is not the end. We live in a dream disguised as a nightmare disguised as a dream. But I can't seem to muscle that courage into words that they can absorb and carry with them as they need them when I am no longer around. Maybe it's just not that time. Or maybe I don't yet lounge in the peace and faith that I profess to play in. Can acceptance be worked on? As in upping the number of steel plates you bench press. Or does it slide in under cover as wisdom does in living the axiomatic well-lived life.

There was a controversial op-ed that came out a few years back by Dr. Richard Smith called "Dying of cancer is the best death."[351] "I often ask audiences how they want to die," Smith would write, "and most people chose sudden death. 'That may be OK for you,' he'd explain, "but it may be very tough on those around you, particularly if you leave an important relationship wounded and unhealed." Smith isn't incorrect. This premonition of me leaving my loved ones behind in the earthly ramshackle of inhabiting a broken heart in a broken city in a broken world is one of the heaviest feelings I have. There's no Hallmark Channel upside in the thinking of your kids having to learn the ropes in the absence of your presence. I've been there as a fatherless child. It's just a sad goddamn thing. A sad fucking thing. But is there, like Smith argues, a gift in the haunt that's been given? Or what psychologists refer to as "post-traumatic growth."[352]

"This is what I learned at the hospital," explained Bradley Cooper's character, Pat, in the movie *Silver Linings Playbook*."[353] "You have to do everything you can, you have to work your hardest, and if you do, if you stay positive, you have a shot at a silver lining." Cooper had just gotten out of an inpatient psychiatric facility, and part of what he meant by working hard was the "therapeutic process." He had suffered loss. He was stuck in a nostalgic madness and was trying to leave that netherworld. He yearned to let go. To accept. It's very much where I'm at. Or where I've been.

"Now, I will never have peace of mind," I said to my mom not long after I found out I had brain cancer. "You never had peace of mind," she replied. Ouch. She was right, though, as uncomfortable as it sounded. I was never exactly a free spirit. But it doesn't mean she's predestined to stay right. She doesn't want to. "I just want you to find peace," my mom would say to me later on. We both cried. In the pit of that sadness—or in the purity in letting the sad just be sad—there was calm, like an eye of a hurricane holds a whisper amidst the swirls of breakage and screams. She, too, has had a go of it. She is still standing, though, and staring up. Definitely more Godot than Galileo. Cleveland born and bred. Cleveland tough. A woman who worked her way up in the shadows to executively assist the executives as they basked in the glow of the clapping and the pats on their back. Never wanting more than she deserved. But getting less than she deserved. The worker's plight. The life of a Clevelander.

I envision a stretch of peace for her even after I am gone. I envision a stretch of peace for her where all the bramble has been cleared and where the glory still stands before the sheen was covered in rust. Psychologically, she and my father have never been apart. She never let go. Never remarried. Whether that is right or wrong is beyond me to judge. It's beyond anyone to judge. It is right in that it exists, and it exists in its rightness.

I remember when I got diagnosed, I was adamant that healing would happen. Or that acceptance would flower like a flower in spring. I wrote on Facebook on January 10th , 2021 that: "In many ways, what this week has brought me and family is a gift. My father died suddenly in a car accident in his early 40's. Looking back, the pain of the loss that echoed forward was in the fuel of all that was left unthought, undone, and unsaid. My family, friends, and myself have already begun this process of discovery. Chewing through not only what if? but what next? Nothing will be left on the table. All will be bitten, tasted, and chewed.

Fast forward to today, and we don't talk about the hard stuff too much. To take one example, a few days after the confirmation of my cancer recurrence, my wife, Andiara, and myself decided to have a sit down with the kids, Angel, 12, Iara, 9, and Artur, 6. We would be telling them that my cancer was actively back and would need more surgery and treatment. We had food. Everything was planned. But the kids didn't want to hear it. They wanted to play Roblox: a game that simulated life. My wife got frustrated. I got frustrated at her frustration. She got frustrated at my frustration at her frustration. The souring mood made tougher an already-impossible topic. And then soon enough the family nucleus began peeling away from what could always be our next-to, next-to, next-to last supper until I was the last one left. Nothing was chewed let alone digested. Instead, it was just me staring at the food that sat in the still-life fashion of Cézanne. There, I sat. Alone at the dinner table. Still in life. But also stilled... in life. Envisioning a time and a place in a Rust Belt city where the family lives on without me. I am trying to prepare for what's next and to gently nudge my family toward this side of the divine as I get whispered over by those who crossed before me. But it seems like an impossible task. It's like being in two places at once. Or being nowhere and doing nothing and in somewhere and doing something.

When you are told you have to let go and accept, what does that mean? At least for me it meant and means leaning heavily on my intellectual and professional experience which, over time, has scaffolded into a conceptual framework that I use to make sense of the senseless if only to put me back on a path that guided me through the valleys and highlands of a worldview through which I viewed the world. The process entailed looking at the literature, reading metanalysis, and deciphering what the problem and point of intervention was and then comparing the outcomes of said interventions after the fact. More exactly, I leaned heavily on my background in clinical psychology, particularly the subfields of psychoanalytic, or depth, psychology. In this discipline, acceptance proceeded through the tending toward personal awareness that'd help me burrow beyond grief and lead me toward the light at the end of the tunnel. This process of heightened consciousness is called integration or, alternatively, individuation, which is essentially processing what's unprocessed and feeling what's unfelt, with the rationale being that what's not weighing you down can't stop you from rising up. Or what's not stuck in your past can't keep you from the present.

"In the broadest possible way," explain the authors of the article "Jung and his Individuation Process" in *Journal Psyche*, "individuation can be defined as the achievement of self-actualization through a process of integrating the conscious and the unconscious."[354] More plainly, if it is unhidden it can't hurt you. And if it's unhurt it can't stop from healing. A friend recently asked, "Do you ever forget?" She meant do I ever forget I have a terminal illness. "All the time," I replied. "Every chance I get." After all, being acutely aware of something, like one's approaching death, is only possible if a state of dulled awareness exists. The average dead man walking is only obtusely, or dimly, or numbingly aware of their inevitabilities. And that's just fine for the most part. You can't walk around with a guillotine necklace and expect to smell the roses. Things can go sideways, however, if what's shoved in is done so inharmoniously and compactfully that the psychic energy that's there gets pressure cooked, inevitably, then, bursting out like a sprung spring so that it becomes "displaced"[355] —to use a Freudian term—onto the other, usually unwelcomingly. When an irate "Karen," for instance, is screaming about mask mandates at some poor cashier at Victoria's Secret who is just trying to ring up pre-dirty underwear for purchase, it's not the mask Hurricane Karen hates but the vulnerability and death that necessitates the mask's existence. But Karen is oblivious to this. Thus, her shittiness to those in the path of her subconsciously-derived low-pressure system.

A few days after my cancer recurrence, I went to my kids' first organized soccer game and Artur and Iara played so well, and I felt such joy. The night before, we went to a high school football game and I watched Angel, my pre-teen 6th-grader and cheerleader-in-training, make the moves into adulthood and then we went to get ice cream, and I felt such joy. A few days after that I screamed, "We won, we won," holding my boy in my arms as the Browns' rookie kicker, Cade York, nailed a 58-yard field goal as time expired, and I felt such joy. The ticking time bomb in my head does get stilled when I allow to be unbothered by the length of the fuse. Call it "acceptance." Call it "piece of mind." Or call it, as philosopher Allan Watts cogently did, "the wisdom of insecurity."[356] Or just call it "life." "Because life is...a flowing proces, writes Watts,"change and death are its necessary parts. To work for their their exclusion is to work against life."

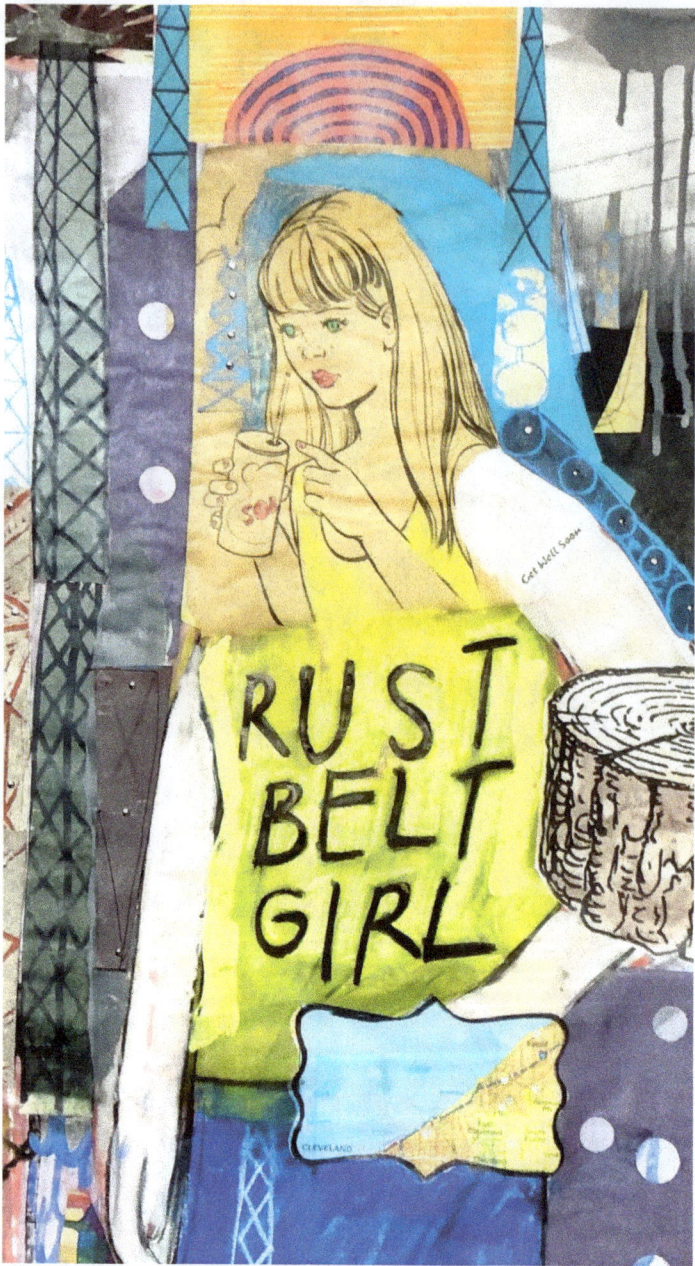

Painting, "Geography and the Body"

Progress Traps, Snap Crap, and a Plasma Bank Called Freedom

When I am wearing my city-building, academic, and/or policy-making hat, there are a few maxims I live by that anchor and frame my worldview when I am trying to glean why the Clevelands of the world are the Clevelands of the world and what a Rust Belt life after death looks like. These maxims go something like this. What's macro becomes micro. What's global becomes local. What's upstream flows downstream. And then from all of these organizing adages a practicality: What's big and abstract is made manifest in what's small and concretized on a given city block. Or what's celllularized in a given person's mind and body.

This conceptualizing view is hardly new. In the summer of 1968 in the Austrian mountain hamlet of Alpbach, author-philosopher Arthur Koestler assembled a who's who of thinkers for a symposium meant to push back against "the insufficient liberation of the life sciences from the mechanistic concepts of nineteenth-century physics and the resulting crudely reductionist philosophy."[357] In other words, Koestler and colleagues had had enough of mind being divorced from matter. The brain, specifically, is not just a meat machine that inputs observation and spits out thoughts and behaviors. It is also a filter of experience that has its own dialect with the body through the mind.

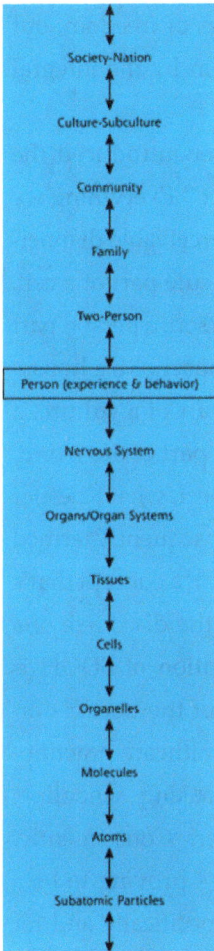

Society-Nation

Culture-Subculture

Community

Family

Two-Person

Person (experience & behavior)

Nervous System

Organs/Organ Systems

Tissues

Cells

Organelles

Molecules

Atoms

Subatomic Particles

It is not just you are what you eat, it is also you are what you feel, or don't feel, if only because the feeling disturbs you. What came out of the meeting—according to Kurt Stange, editor of *Annals of Family Medicine* in the essay "The Science of Connectedness"[358] —was "a chain of evidence that biological and social phenomena, like molecular and physical occurrences, evolve as events with many degrees of freedom, but with 'ordering restraints exerted upon them by the integral activity of the 'whole.'"

A year prior to the convening, Koestler introduced the idea of a holon, designated as a "whole part." Everything we categorize as matter is linked, despite its perceivable distinctness. An atom is part of a molecule, a molecule part of a cell, a cell part of an organ, an organ part of a person, a person part of a relationship, a relationship part of a household, a household part of a community, a community part of a culture, a culture part of a nation-state, a nation-state part of the world, and the world part of the cosmos. In retrospect, what Koestler and his ilk were driving at is what's been subsequently termed the "social determinants of health" (SDOH):[359] a concept that's moved from the borders of academia into the discourse of a general consensus. The shorthand explanation of SDOH is that 80% of one's health happens outside of the doctor's office, with the other 20% in the hands of healthcare practitioners. Put another way, issues like food, housing, schooling, smoking, psychosocial stress, etc., matter. Consequently, SDOH has become a hot-button topic that's proving to be a looking glass for the healthcare industry specifically and for the American experiment generally—particularly that balance between economic development and societal progress, or a fiscally robust healthcare industry sucking on the teat of a sick patient population.

This need for self-reflection has been boiling over for some time now. "Our national accounting system, or Gross Domestic Product (GDP) counts things like imprisonment, air pollution, war production, cigarette ads, gun purchases", explained Robert Kennedy in 1968. "Yet it does not allow for the health of our children, the strength of our marriages, the intelligence of our public debate. It measures everything...except that which makes life worthwhile."[360]

There is a little strip mall on the corner of E. 156th St. and Lakeshore Blvd., not a stone's throw from my house that contains a Georgio's Oven Fresh Pizza, a daycare center, and a plasma bankcalled "Freedom." That Freedom exists in that particular spot is neither random nor intelligently designed. I live in Cleveland's East Side in a section of the neighborhood of North Collinwood that is over 70% Black and has a poverty rate creeping up to 50%.[361] For those not in the know, plasma banks are places where people go to sell their blood from which plasma is extracted through intermediaries, such as Freedom, to be sold at scale to pharmaceutical companies for various research and development purposes so it ultimately translates into high-end products that can be sold on the knowledge economy market. What's a knowledge economy? The OECD definition describes it as "trends in advanced economies towards greater dependence on knowledge, information and high skill levels, and the increasing need for ready access to all of these by the business and public sectors."[362] Put another way, instead of tangible, or touchable, assets— e.g., raw materials, machinery, physical labor—fueling economic growth, a knowledge economy is powered by intangible assets, like ideas, ingenuity, and intellectual labor.

Freedom Plasma in North Collinwood.

Source: Richey Piiparinen

As knowledge increasingly takes centerstage in the global market, knowledge industries, including next-generation extractive sectors, like plasma banking, are becoming big business. As noted in the 2021 investigative report "Blood Money" by NPR's Amanda Aronczyk, sales in the globalized plasma industry are around $25 billion a year, and two-thirds of the world's plasma supply comes from the United States.[363] Two-thirds is a big number. The U.S. no longer exports two-thirds of anything. Do Americans have an abundance of plasma, like the largest global cheese exporter, Germany, has an abundance of Limburger? No. It's far less commendable and artisanal than that. The World Health Organization—after the disaster that was the Sandinistas creating a 24-hour town in

Nicaragua known for plasma harvesting nicknamed "Casa de Vampiros" — came out with a blanket declaration against paying for plasma, particularly given the inevitability that the process would take advantage of the marginalized. Just about every country globally fell in line with that WHO declaration, including Nicaragua. There was, however, one exception. The U.S. [364] Hence, the Freedom Plasma at the corner of my street. Against this backdrop, the name "Freedom Plasma" couldn't be more Orwellian if it tried. No matter. A question: If the hypothetical you, the run-of-the-mill market Libertarian, were running a mom-and-pop plasma center and longed for a turnstile-type operation for blood-banking, where would you put it? Well, near the source of supply, the characteristics of which include places with rampant macroeconomic displacement threaded with a widespread urge to scrape by. Where better than a high-poverty, majority minority neighborhood in a Rust Belt city? "You can think of blood plasma as a kind of strange version of a natural resource," Aronczyk continues in her investigative report, "like it's trees or iron or whatever. So, in that metaphor, the plasma collection centers are the places where you extract that resource. It's the forest or the mine."[365] Now, does that sound like progress? i.e., the veins of a human body acting as topographical canals to juice the global economy with the blood of the run-down? Of course not. It's downright backwards, in fact. And that's exactly the point. It's a point that will be unraveled as this essay stretches out to reveal just how warped our sense of progress has become, including our ability to gauge whether a given city has succeeded as a society or not.

What Aronczyk is getting at when she compares the plasma bank to a lumber yard or coal mine is the notion that the global economy, like everything, is fluid. And it evolves, or matures, as the value-add of a given economic era changes along with the general-purpose technologies of the times. There are not a few conceptual models out there that explain this change. But one I found helpful in my teaching and research is a model by economists Fisher and Clark called the "Four Sector Theory."[366] It explains that the global economy had a "Primary" stage that was natural resource-driven (circa 1800s), leading to a "Secondary" stage that was industrially-driven (circa 1940s), followed by a "Tertiary" stage which is one of service provision. In Cleveland, this meant an economy backstopped by the likes of Rockefeller's Standard Oil in the late 1800s, to Ford in the mid-20th century, to Cleveland Clinic today. The latest, most emergent stage, "Quaternary," is all about the cutting-edges of technology. Think big data, computer processing, "the cloud," and artificial intelligence. "As evidenced by the economic development history of mankind from an agricultural to an industrial and finally to a service economy is a natural and inevitable process for a specific country and even for the whole," explains one international economist, noting that the United States—though a later arrival to the Industrial Revolution compared to Europe—was "the first country to shift to a 'service economy' in the middle of the twentieth century."[367]

It's a shift, however, that has landed hardest on the backs of the working class. Think about the union pipefitter who has been relegated to toiling the aisles of Home Depot and answering home improvement questions about fitting pipes. The easiest way to show this evolutionary restructuring is to chart Manufacturing versus Service sector jobs across time. Between 1969 and 2000, the divergence in employment between goods production and service provision is obvious. Cleveland's Cuyahoga County, for instance, lost nearly 154,000 Manufacturing jobs, yet gained about 169,000 Service jobs. But not all service jobs are created equal.

In fact, a bifurcation in the labor market between higher-wage knowledge economy jobs, and lower-wage service jobs has taken place in the U.S., in effect metamorphosizing the playing field of the American dream into a buzz saw that splits well-being via employment opportunities between those attached to the knowledge economy and those not. Elaborating, knowledge economy jobs proliferating include occupations in education, healthcare, information technology; and professional service positions, including those in finance, real estate, and management. Conversely, the lower-wage service jobs include the likes of retail, leisure and hospitality, janitorial, housekeeping, and administrative support. And lest we forget the proverbial gig economy workers that provide the labor supply that feed the profits of Big Tech,[368] sans worker benefits or

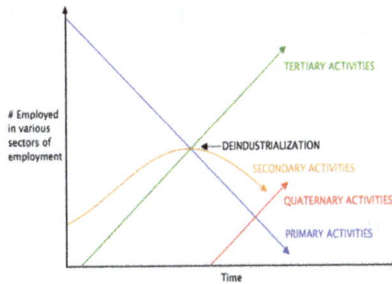

Clark and Fisher Four Sector Theory

job security. "National survey of gig workers paints a picture of poor working conditions, low pay," headlines a 2021 report from the Economic Policy Institute.[369]

Total Private Sector Employment in Cuyahoga County that is in the Manufacturing, or Secondary, Sector and Service, or Tertiary Sector.

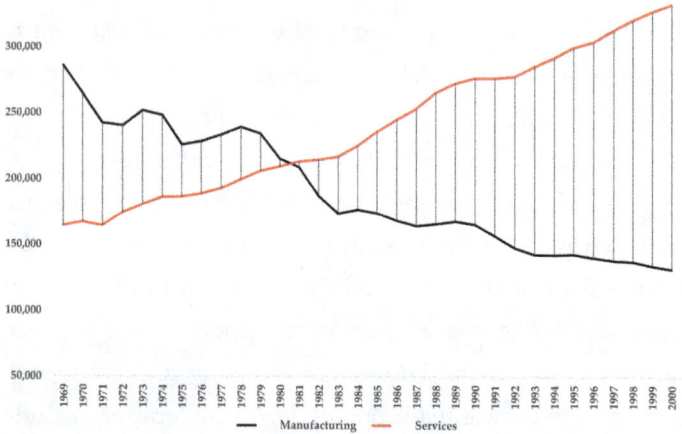

Source: BEA, CAEMP25S, 1969-2000.

Okay, so what does this all mean? The takeaway? Well, we got progress, or an economic evolution from Manufacturing to Services that began some time back, dislocating Rust Belt workers from living wages. MIT's David Autor recently showed that much of the working class didn't "graduate" into knowledge economy work, but instead became subsistent on lower-wage service work. A "barbelling" of the labor market thus ensued, with knowledge workers on one end and service workers on the other.[370] An early sermonizer of the term "knowledge economy,"[371] famed management theorist Peter Drucker envisioned such a scenario. "Knowledge workers and service workers are not 'classes' in the traditional sense..." Peter Drucker wrote in his book *Post-Capitalist Society*. "But there is a danger that ... society will become a class society unless service workers attain both income and dignity."[372] Pre-COVID-19, the scholarly argument for service worker wage stagnation was that pay was commensurate with returns to skill. The wage premiums are for those in the techne class, or for the arbiters of knowledge economy, as they provide the value-add in the current economic era. That's true.[373] But only partly, as that valuation came to coincide with a devaluation of manual, last-mile work as an unglamorous, rudimentary endeavor, so explains the New York Times' Thomas Edsall in his aggregation of the latest wage/worker findings in the analysis, "Why Do We Pay So Many People So Little Money?"[374]

Yet COVID-19 exposed that devaluation as a self-serving fallacy.[375] Matter of fact, as telecommuting normalizes and knowledge workers work from home in the safety of physical separateness, they can only do so if the necessities brought to their doorstep—e.g., sanitation, food, utilities—are, in fact, brought. If not, the knowledge stops. This reality is increasingly being realized thanks to the backhanded wakeup call that was the plague. In his daily letters to his staff dated April 8th, 2020, for instance, Craig R. Smith, the Chair of the Department of Surgery in New York City's Columbia Medical Center, discussed the risk associated with transporting COVID-19 patients from the ER in the infectious disease wing, noting the orderlies are selflessly stepping up. His concluding paragraph reads:

> Transport is just one reminder that every contribution matters. Consider this admirably prideful Tweet from "Jester D" on March 14: 'I'm a garbageman. I can't work from home and my job is an essential city service that must get done…. Doctors and nurses are going to keep doctoring and nurse-ering. Us garbagemen are gonna keep collecting the garbage.' Indeed, it

must get done. Singer-songwriter John Prine died of COV-ID-19 yesterday, at age 73. He worked a day job as a mail carrier in Chicago for five years early in his career. John Prine wrote songs for common people… 'The scientific nature of the ordinary man / Is to go out and do the best you can.'[376]

Crucially, the split in the labor market between knowledge work vs. service work is not only evident as an upstream macro factor, the bifurcation proceeds down-stream to make an imprint in a city's neighborhoods as well. This is what I mean when I say what's global is local or what's macro is micro. Specifically, the maps below show Cuyahoga County's Lower-wage Service workers are residentially concentrated in predominantly Black, lower-income neighborhoods with lower educational attainment rates and lower rates of internet access. In other words, the bifurcation of the regional labor market is manifested as a bifurcation of the local housing market, a phenomenon called "residential sorting" by urban economists.[377] Knowledge workers, by contrast, have clustered in Cleveland's urban core, as well as near Cleveland's hospitals and universities, or its University Circle neighborhood.

Where Lower-wage Service Workers live in Cuyahoga County.

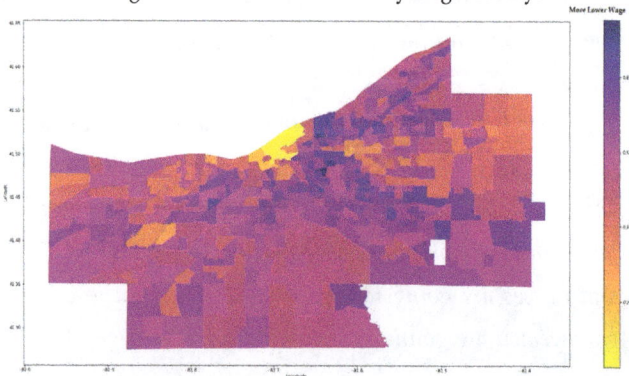

Source: LODES2020 Author's calculations.

Black Residents

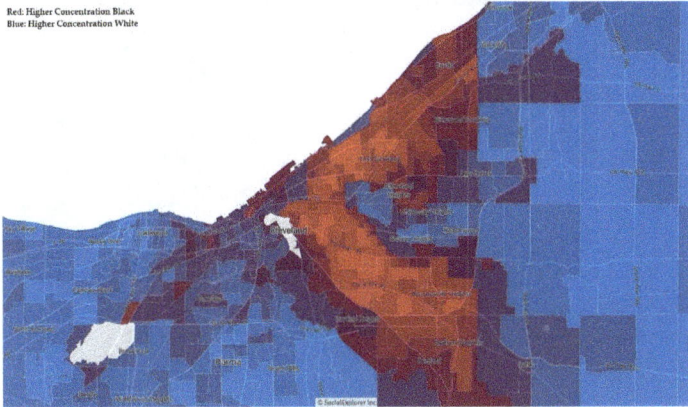

Source: ACS 5-Year 2019. Note: Redder = higher
concentration Black residents

Educational Attainment, Bachelor's or higher

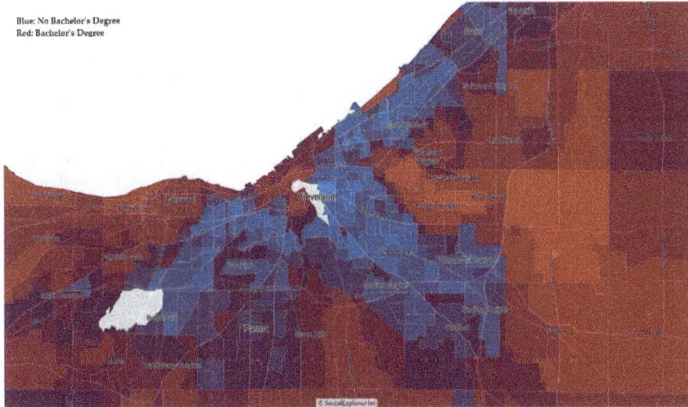

Source: ACS 5-Year 2019. Note: Redder = higher concentration college edu-
cated.

Where Lower-wage Service Workers live in Cuyahoga County.

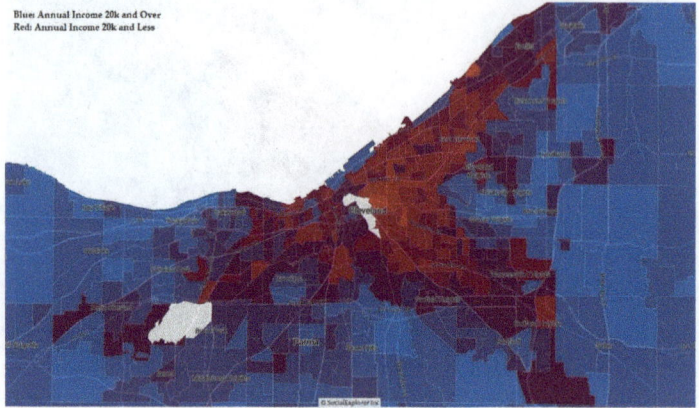

Source: LODES2020 Author's calculations

Percent Households No Internet Access.

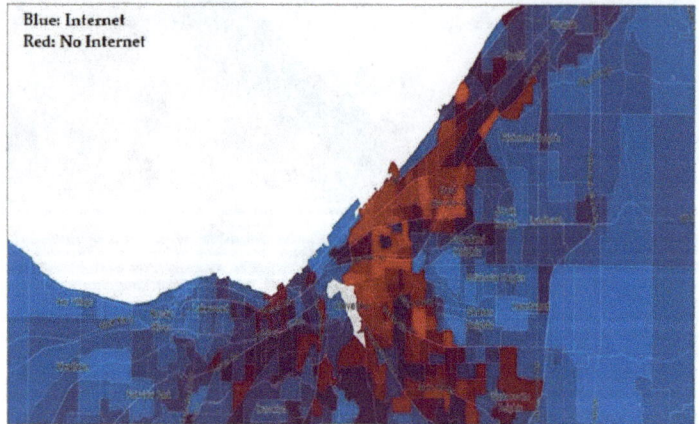

Source: ACS 5-Year 2019.
Note: Redder = higher concentration No Internet

Inevitably, the demographic sorting, then, gets played out in the way amenities flow. Knowledge- and tech-worker neighborhoods are flush with investment, manifest as a cornucopia of goods and services that check-off Maslow's hierarchy of needs: physical safety, healthy food, clean air and water, quality housing, good schools and healthcare, pretty aesthetics and parks, a strong social fabric and concomitant information access, not to mention the freedom from scarcity that allows the luxury of aspiration. Meanwhile, disamenities grow in areas of isolation: violence and trauma, dirty air and water, deteriorating housing, poor schools and health services, a social bond break with less information and support, and a lack of a psychological and spiritual reprieve that comes with perpetually existing without enough.

The spatial split brings to mind a book by Thomas P.M. Barnett's called *The Pentagon's New Map*.[378] For the expert geostrategist, the world is divided between two types of geographies: the "Core," where "globalization is thick with network connectivity, financial transactions, liberal media flows, and collective security" and the "Gap," or areas disconnected from globalization and defined by poverty, low education rates and "the chronic conflicts that incubate the next generation" of instability.[379] While Barnett's "haves and have nots" was conceived at the level of the nation-state, it need not stay there. There is a Core and Gap between American regions, within regions, and between and within neighborhoods. "We ignore the Gap's existence at our own peril," concludes Barnett.

Ultimately, the sorting between amenity-rich and -poor communities ends up landing in the geography of the body. This is evidenced in the map below showing the spatial inheritances of life expectancy in Cuyahoga County. Lower life expectancy clusters in space as if it were a contagion. In many respects, it is. The field of epigenetics, for example, shows how the environment, or the outside, modifies a person's DNA, or the inside.[380] That is, structural economic changes globally manifest as socioeconomic inequalities locally, igniting psychosocial stress that changes the body's biology and, in turn, its life expectancy trajectory.

Life Expectancy in Cuyahoga County

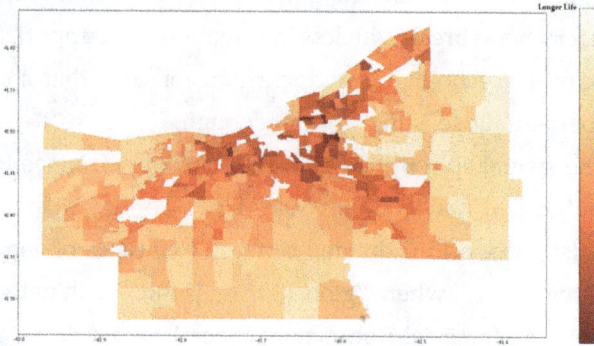

Source: U.S. Small-area Life Expectancy Estimates Project – USALEEP, 2010-2015. Author's calculations.

It's a sequence that lingers intergenerationally. "Each exposure has effects that may persist across the life course and in some instances may be transmitted to offspring via epigenetic inheritance," notes the authors of the essay "Biological memories of past environments: Epigenetic pathways to health disparities."[381] "Since epigenetic markings provide a 'memory' of past experiences, minimizing future disparities in health will be partially contingent upon our ability to address inequality in the current environment."[382] For the most part, this is not being done. Healthcare is often an after-the-fact industry, treating bodily disease as opposed to the "upstream" impacts on the body. That's not surprising. Health practitioners can only do so much. They can treat sick individuals, but sick societies? That's not up them. It's up to "us."

Regardless, what's occurring isn't exactly working. In 1970, life expectancy in the U.S (70.8) ranked 18th out of 43 peer nations.[383] With the latest figures from the OECD, U.S. life expectancy today (77) ranks 32nd , one spot behind Communist China.[384] This, despite the U.S. spending $11,859 per capita annually in healthcare services—by far the most among developed nations.[385] This discordance is plotted below. Most countries with high spends have higher life expectancies. Not in America. The nation stands exceedingly alone, despite having the best medical institutions in the world. Institutions like Mayo, MD Anderson, Cleveland Clinic, Sloan Kettering, Johns Hopkins that patients from all over the world travel to in an attempt to stay alive. The best technologies but not the best outcomes. What's going on? At the risk of sounding pithy, the knowledge economy, as we constructed it, is demonstrably dumb.

Life Expectancy at Birth Vs. Health Spending Per Capita,

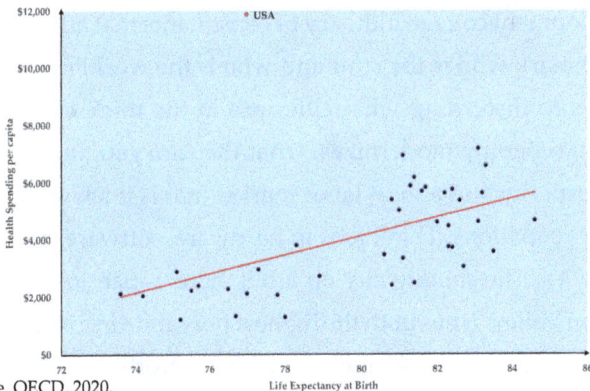

Source, OECD, 2020.

In Daniel Brian O'Leary's *Escaping the Progress Trap*,[386] the "progress trap" is defined as "conditions advanced economies find themselves in when science, technology and industry create more problems than they can solve. Often inadvertently."[387] Think a Kurt Vonnegut novel. But in real life. Progress traps pockmark civilization's march forward, and they seemingly do so now more than ever. Ecological calamities come to mind. As do disinformation campaigns that ride shotgun with our hyper connectedness and thirst for novelty. Who needs post-modernism when we can cosplay in post-truth? Hell, QAnon nihilists make the deconstructionist philosopher Foucault look like Fouwhatever.[388] "Knowledge is not made for understanding," demanded Foucault, "it is made for cutting." [389]

Given my vocation centers around understanding how cities like Cleveland evolve, I've come to focus on the progress trap(s) that coincide with cities' economic development efforts. A few barometers of progress have become standard-bearers as to whether or not a given city has suitably died or sustained commercial life, namely per capita income and tech job concentration. That is, as city leaders and the economic development cottage industry of consultants that advise them benchmark who is the stud and who is the weakling when it comes to discerning what cities are in the thick of it as the global economy modernizes, what they are gauging, in part, is prosperity and a local labor market that is thick with high-tech occupations. Think jobs in hardware, software, and data analytics. The shining city on a hill, here, is San Jose, CA, or Silicon Valley. It has both the highest per capita income among the nation's largest 40 metros, with its Northern California cousin, San Francisco, second. San Jose also has the highest concentration of jobs in mathematical and computer occupations.[390] Given such metrics, Silicon Valley has entered into its own stratosphere of achievement which, in turn, has made it the geography of aspiration: a veritable North Star of economic progress. This has led to the inescapable copycat strategy to become "the next Silicon Valley." Ethernet inventor Robert Metcalfe wrote in 1998 that "Silicon Valley is the only place on earth not trying to figure out how to become Silicon Valley."[391] This often entails a place-branding campaign to christen a part of one's city as Silicon "X." For example, Philadelphia had branded part of its city as "Philicon Valley," whereas New York has "Silicon Alley." New Orleans has "Silicon Bayou" and Portland has "Silicon Forest." There's "Silicon Swamp" in Gainesville, "Silicon Slopes" in Utah, "Silicon Harbor" in Charleston, and a variant of "Silicon Prairie" in Dallas, Chicago, Omaha, and Jackson Hole, Wyoming.[392] Here in Ohio, with the arrival of Intel and its semiconductor manufacturing plant, the words "Silicon Heartland" [393] have rolled off the lips of not a few state officials, usually at a ribbon cutting while holding the obligatory goldish shovel.

Real Per Capita Income (in 2012$) for Largest 40 Metros

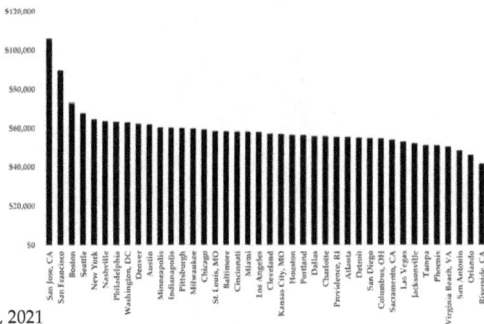

Source: BEA, 2021

Okay, this is what's recognized and remembered about Silicon Valley: It's flush with prosperity and the pieces parts of a cutting-edge, quaternary economy. What's less known is that San Jose and San Francisco also lead the nation in measures of disparity, as documented in the 2022 analysis by this author called "Disrupting Innovation." San Jose has the second largest income gap between White and Black residents among big-city metros, trailing only San Francisco. [394] It also ranked worst in a statistic called the 90/10 wage ratio, or the gap between what the wealthiest 10 percent in a region makes versus the poorest 10%. [395]

As the scatterplots below show, this relationship between prosperity and disparity is less a bug than a feature of the modern economy. Looking at all metros nationally, there is a statistically robust positive relationship between how prosperous a city is and how disparate it is when it comes to income by race. As well, the more a city's economy is rife with tech occupations, the more the city is unequal when it comes to wage inequality, with San Jose, CA a posterchild for these paradoxes of progress.

Per Capita Income and Income Gaps by Race for All U.S. Metros.

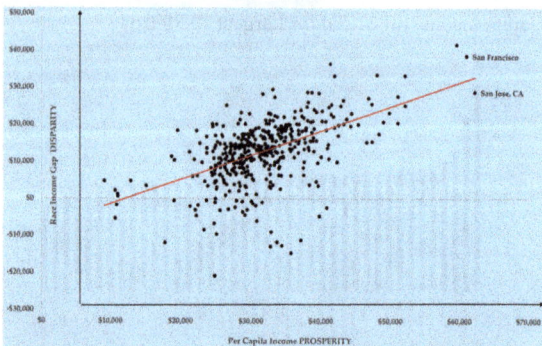

Source: ACS 1-Year, 2020.

Share of computer and Mathematical Employment vs. 90/10 Wage Ratio by Metro.

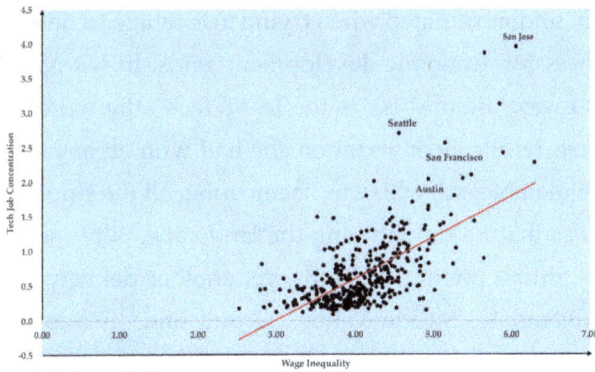

Source: OES, May 2020.

This, folks, is what is meant by a progress trap. We have a system in which economic progress coincides with—if not engenders—a societal regress. Why? Two recent reports help unpack the issue. In a January 2022 *New York Times* piece entitled "Economists Pin More Blame on Tech for Rising Inequality," [396] the author interviews MIT's Daron Acemoglu whose research showed at least half of the gap in American's wages over the last 40 years was due to "excessive automation [of work]," particularly work done by men without college degrees. Given less than one-third of men in the U.S. have a college degree (the figure is 18.6% in the City of Cleveland), that's a lot of displaced workers. The effects hit communities of color particularly hard. One report, "The Future of Work in Black America," noted that Black workers are 10% more at risk for job disruption due to automation, with that number rising to nearly 30% for Black men without a college degree.[397] Modern market practices, or using innovation to excessively displace workers is "not an act of God or nature," continues MIT's Acemoglu. "It's the result of choices…we as a society have made about how to use technology."

I think the phrase "how to use technology" is vital and wholly underexamined when trying to leverage technological advances for economic development gains. In her *New York Times* essay "Elon Musk Is the Id of Tech" the writer, Kara Swisher, recalls a conversation she had with an angel investor, Pejman Nozad, who was "bemoaning all the stupid start-up ideas that he saw littering the landscape. Silly social networks, dumb photo filter apps, yet another delivery service for millennials. 'Silicon Valley,' Nozad said, 'is a lot of big minds chasing small ideas.'" [398]

Enter Snap Crap. It wasn't long back that San Francisco was seen as the golden child of the tech-driven urban renaissance.[399] San Francisco was, after all, replete with a real-deal, cool vibe; great restaurant, art, and music scenes, and a cosmopolitan feel that had beatnik wannabes hitchhiking back for more. And those bouncy balls used as desk chairs. Now, with its rampant inequality parting the waters as a macro factor, what's showing up downstream is the piling up of human feces in the commons. "A city covered in poop is so disgusting it has to be almost comical," begins *The Guardian*'s Nathan Robinson in his piece "Why is San Francisco covered in human feces."[400] "But the uptick in street defecation is the symbol of a human tragedy," Robinson continues, "People aren't pooping on the streets because they have suddenly forgotten what a bathroom is, or unlearned basic hygiene. The incidents are part of a broader failure of the city to provide for the basic needs of its citizens, and show the catastrophic, socially destructive effects of unchecked inequality."[401]

The answer? It is, perhaps predictably, a crowd-sourced

app named "Snap Crap" that—according to its developer—allows residents of San Francisco to "request street and side-walk cleaning from the city's Public Works department by submitting a photo of something gross (usually crap) and sharing its location."[402]

California dreaming this ain't.

Which brings us to another maxim I live by when I am trying to course correct Cleveland and other Rust Belt cities out of the well-worn path of policy copycatting and collective depravity. It goes: A society that functions flows into the physical and mental welfare of its citizens which, in turn, feeds back into the functioning of society. A society that doesn't, doesn't. Meaning that technotopia of a city mythically found on the coastal U.S. is not a model for inland aspirations. Nor is it a model, for that matter, for coastal aspiraions. The formula for building a city is almost too simple—embarrassingly so—when it comes to the conceptual scaffolding of a workable strategic frame for policymakers. Take care of your people. Manufacture well-being.[403] The rest—i.e., civic pride, a city brand—will take care of itself.

Charcoal and Pastel Sketch, "Manufactures Well-being,"

The Skull,
Spacetime,
and the
Soul of a City

I was a stranger in a strange land. A potato bug below the thumb of a giant, under the best of circumstances. An ant behind the magnifying glass of a latchkey kid, otherwise. "There's little healing in this," I kept thinking as I laid in the dark, the echoes of code red and code violet greasing through the halls of the hospital, like the sound of a train whistle coursing through a carless tunnel. "If anything, there's healing from this." I closed my eyes. I was dog-tired but couldn't rest. My stomach was yelling but couldn't eat. There are few places, after all, more surreal than the neuro ICU wing in a big-city hospital. I feel qualified to surmise. This is my third time in one. Two craniotomies and a traumatic brain injury, the latter occurring after tumbling into the windshield of an oncoming car on W. 25th St. near Downtown Cleveland. The former occurring after being baptized with brain malignancy.

The Skull. Sculpture by Mike "Mac" McNamara

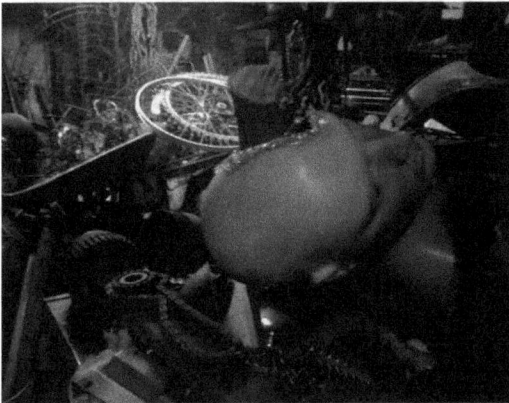

Photo by Richey Piiparinen

If it wasn't for the protective functioning of the cranium, I'd be slop. As would you. That's because while each of us is unique, a universality we share is having a shell, or skull, sheathing our brains. The brain: that house of the mind. The mind: that house of the soul. The soul: that house of the spirit. The spirit: that house of transcendence. Transcendence: that house of making meaning in the face of what's meaningless. Meaning: that house of having put together what's been brought to pieces.

"The skull is anterior to the spinal column and is the bony structure that encases the brain," explains Medline.[404] "Its purpose is to protect the brain and allow attachments for the facial muscles."

One of those muscles was throbbing as I lay. My right temporalis muscle, also known as the temporal muscle, or one of the muscles of chewing that's located in front of the ear, had to be "dissected," said the neurosurgery resident. "In contemporary neurosurgery, when performing a pterional craniotomy, neurosurgeons have been taught to cut through and detach the temporalis before drilling the skull to turn a bone flap," explain the authors of the article, "Effect of Crani-otomy on Temporalis Function."[405] They did this so as to re-sect the recurrent tumor in my right temporal lobe. It worked, as much as anything does with a so-far cureless affliction. They got what they needed to get out, though, including clearing up the original resection cavity of necrosis, or zombie tissue, in the right occipital lobe. But the discomfort was for real. To keep my spirits up, I tried to contextualize my state of affairs with our state of affairs. I am not alone. We are in this together. This experience of mine is but one drop in oceans of human experience under the tide of a blood-moon millennia, one exemplified by another ubiquity: pain, both physical and mental. "There is a great deal of pain in life," notes the famed

Scottish psychiatrist R.D. Laing, "and perhaps the only pain that can be avoided is the pain that comes from trying to avoid pain."[406] Imagine pain as a rubber ball in your hand. The harder you throw it away, the harder it bounces back. In psychology, this is called "the rebound effect" defined as "an intensification of behavior following a period of repression." [407]

"Richard, don't get out of bed," the man's voice kept saying. It was deep into the night. The witching hour in time. A cuckoo's nest in space. The voice seemed to be coming from above. How the man knew I was moving, I don't know. "But I have to use the bathroom," I thought, the catheter they put in days ago about as useful as a gutter cut in half. So, I tried again to get up. The toilet was right there. But the man clapback, his tone more exasperated than angry. "Richard, don't get out of bed." They didn't want me to fall. This went on for 50 minutes. At one point two nurses came in to remove the catheter, with one remarking to the other, "It's hanging by a thread." I didn't know what she meant but think it explained its dysfunction.

The next night I got a visitor, despite the validity of the predicament the night prior. She was not wearing scrubs and pulled a chair up to the foot of my bed. She was a bigger, Black lady and said very little, but I sensed she was the no-nonsense type by the aura she exuded. "I am your sitter," she exclaimed, staring at the floor. "I heard you kept getting up last night." "Wut?" I thought. "I mean, I'm not here to cause a fuss. I am not here. Here, I am not. Where am I?"

Not a day ago, I was not there. I was at home, having been released from the ICU a few days out of brain surgery. But not long after I got home, I started seeing things. A cat that wasn't

there. Ants climbing in a layer on the white panels of the din-
ing room wall. A Pixar project was projecting out of my head.
My wife whizzed me out of there at the encouragement of my
mom, both of us leaving behind the ashen faces of the kids
who just wanted their old dad back. But I was long gone. Surf-
ing the brain waves of an EEG.

You see, by then the seizures had started, with 'em gaining momentum and force as the sands of the hourglass
dropped. These are the days of our lives. By the time I got inside the ER the battle rumble was on. King Kong Bundy, the
Iron Sheik, Jimmy Superfly, the works. Imagine fighting a
lightning bolt. And then imagine losing. I was being dragged
asunder by invisible forces, zombie ghosts. I was being pulled
away. I was aware I was being pulled away. I was aware of
my awareness of being pulled away. "I don't want to die
here," I said to myself. I don't want to die. I could hear my
wife whimper behind me as a team of ER nurses piled on.
"Turn his head," one screamed. The leader of the pack was a
real Cleveland regular. A bar fly. A *Drew Carey Show* stand-in.
Bigger, White. Dated hairdo. Since I was semi-aware, I later
learned that, technically, I was having a focal seizure. But it
felt like a grand mal. (It was a grand mal.) I never had a seizure as powerful until then. I remember, too, that the Browns
were on TV in the nurses' stations. The game encouraged me
to come to. I was a die-hard. With an emphasis on dying hard.
I asked the orderly that was with me, a younger Black dude,
what the score was. He pumped his fist in the air, as I was
back to reality. He was happy I didn't flame out. "You really
want to know?" he asked, shaking his head to express discon-
tentment. "Yup." "10-3, Atlanta." "Fuck," I said. They were

on a losing streak. Same old Cleveland. The Browns, me, the city. The losses never stop. Fathomless in their procession. Morning after morning: the mourning.

From the ER I was moved back to the neuro ICU, by now coming full circle to where I was before I left. I was, understandably, still in and out, by then on a bevy of meds, including Dilaudid, a strong opiate, and an anti-convulsant drip of Keppra and Vimpat. Not long after I got back there a young Mexican-American nurse who was smiling came up to me, "Richard, do you remember me from last night?" I looked at her quizzingly. "Not really." "You look so much better now," she said. "Really?" I thought.

There was, after all, a newish set of metal staples above my right ear mimicking the look of a zipper of flesh, albeit one keeping the contents of my conscious experience intact. If my brain slips out and goes cold on the floor—a freshly-caught walleye on a Lake Erie break wall losing its flip flop—does my mind go with it? And thus, my soul? And thus, my spirit? And thus, the hope and/or belief that there was meaning in any of this? It better not. I trust I am not alone here. We are in this together. I don't mind dying per se. Or "transitioning" as I'd been desirously calling death lately. It's the forced farewell that kills me, my death releasing the grief forward into the pit of the bellies of those I love desperately and who love me, only to settle in the toiled soil of what's been called the "transcendent function."[408] Or the need in life to unify the pull of the opposites as they wash over you as you go about the business of your lifespan. Polarities such as life and death; yin and yang; hi and bye; hurt and happiness; peace and war; all and nothing. It is not an easy thing to do; that is, to accept a loss so as to gain a gain. To soak in dark so as to bathe in light. Perhaps that's why heaven is such a delicious concept. Who wouldn't want to leave the pitchforks of this place to enter into a spacetime unconfined by the chains of time and space?

These chains. They are our limits. Is existence, for instance, really bounded by four-dimensional space that's rather primitively understood as up, down, left, right? Or north, south, east, west? As well as a dimension called time that is measured by an arrow that goes from past to future through now, with now notoriously unexploited by what is experienced as past through memory and as future through anticipation? I mean, that mental model will get you to work on time before your boss gets pissed, but it won't answer the question of why you go to a job you hate and put off finding the job you love. It just won't. The answer to that question can only be found in the vigorous terrain of one's inner world, i.e., the psyche, with its conscious and unconscious contents. Its sunrise and sea depths. Yet it's an inner world of mind interplayed with an outer world of matter, with the flow in between always changing and purged as moods, motives, relationships, and behaviors. As love and violence, and health and sickness, and bricks and mortar, and blood and guts, and diamonds and lipstick.

In fact, the plausibility of another dimension is gaining traction in numerous domains, like theoretical physics and alternative medicine. "Our Universe may have a fifth dimension that would change everything we know about physics." headlines a *Science Focus* article from 2021.[409] "There is a way to have a bigger fifth dimension," the authors write. "This fifth dimension is curved in such a way that we don't see it,

and this was suggested by the physicists Lisa Randall and Ra-
man Sundrum in 1999. An extra space dimension might even
explain one of the great cosmic mysteries: the identity of 'dark
matter,' the invisible stuff that appears to outweigh the visible
stars and galaxies by a factor of six."[410] The idea of a fifth
dimension has also entered the alternative healing space. The
use of plant-based medicines that induce next-level, psyche-
delic experiences such as ayahuasca and psilocybin are increasingly common, as evidenced by the 2022 Netflix Series
*How to Change Your Mind: What the New Science of Psychedelics
Teaches Us About Consciousness, Dying, Addiction, Depression.*
Written by Cleveland's own best-selling author Michael Pol-
len to rave reviews, *The Guardian*'s write-up explains it thusly:
"Sweeping and often thrilling . . . It is to Pollan's credit that,
while he ranks among the best of science writers, he's willing,
when necessary, to abandon the genre's fixation on materialist explanation as the only path to understanding."[411]

Whether or not there is a fifth dimension that extends beyond Einstein's Theory of Relativity, I am not sure. Neither
am I remotely credentialed to lay the gavel down on either
side of the line, besides. Regardless, what we know about
"this" and "us" is likely far less than we care to admit. These
limitations, then, of understanding how we are, and who we
are, and why we are is not just an individual reality. It's a collective position that's ultimately played out in the norms,
frames of reference, and institutionalized procedures of what
we do, why we do, and how we do. For the sake of these pages, that means how we tend to the sick so as to foster health.
And how we tend to cities so as make fertile societies. Now, I
get it. I can feel you thinking that this is all going out on a limb

that's bending and about to break, leaving this essay, if not the collection as a whole, to the fate of Humpty Dumpty, or all broke in yolk. But that's only because we've been conditioned not to imbue the transcendental with the pragmatic, fleshy, caulked, and concretized. We separate our science, technology, engineering, and mathematics (STEM) from our humanities in the thirst for knowledge and progress, like we do our sauerkraut and kielbasa. In doing so, we separate the application of knowledge from the wisdom of knowledge. And it's a division that's becoming increasingly rotted out.

As noted by the University College of London's Nicholas Maxwell in his article "From Knowledge to Wisdom," [412] the issue boils down to the fact that the human desire to solve the problems of science have not been met with equivalent vigor spent on the problems of living. "It is...of decisive importance to appreciate that all global problems have arisen because of a massive increase in scientific knowledge and technology without a concomitant increase in global wisdom," Maxwell writes. As long as we lacked modern science, the lack of wisdom—described as the capacity to understand what is of value in life for oneself and for others—mattered less, as the ability to wreak havoc was limited. "Now that our power to act has been so massively enhanced by modern science and technology, global wisdom has become, not a luxury, but a necessity."[413] Or as the American naturalist writer Edward O. Wilson put it: "The real problem of humanity is the following: we have paleolithic emotions; medieval institutions; and godlike technology."[414]

The issue extends into city building. The hunch, for instance, that Cleveland, or the Rust Belt, has a psyche and a soul is rarely, if ever, considered or discussed in policy-making, let alone rigorously integrated into methodologies—e.g., urban planning, economic development—that are meant to make a techne out of the revitalization of tottering towns. Rather, it's all nuts and bolts, traffic engineering, master plans, input-output models, and topographical surveys. It's all demolition and erection. But none of the poetry or artisanry that is the exhuming of a city's transcendental qualities. It's arguably the biggest blind spot in the discipline of societal construction and urban settlement, including a place's ruination or revitalization.

"Who cares?", you ask. We do. Because this discipline is not just read about in over-priced, hard cover textbooks and squinted at on chalkboards scribbled on by life-inexperienced professors. Rather, it's lived in. And as such is absorbed and lives in the settler who has settled in, be it restfully or desperately. Healthily or sickly. Industrious or discarded. I once heard one man say to another in a Drug Mart, a drugstore chain in Cleveland, that "you either have a hammer in your hand or you're getting hammered on the head." He meant you're either working or getting worked. He had a loaf of white bread in one hand a twelve pack in the other. I've seen a version of this man and woman, White, Black, Puerto Rican, a thousand times over in the course of my 46 years in Cleveland. It's no doubt the city's most common archetype, comprising a good-sized chunk of the soul of the city: that of the hardscrabble, head-just-above-water blue-collar Cleveland tough.

And though it can be argued that a class is a class, not the attribute of the mystical or soulful, let's let the poetry of John Lennon be the judge. Writes Lennon: "As soon as you're born, they make you feel small. By giving you no time instead of it all, 'Til the pain is so big you feel nothing at all. A working-class hero is something to be."[415]

And the fact that this blind spot is so predominant in city building is ironic, because the oldest human settlements, as thoroughly detailed by Lewis Mumford in his classic *The City in History*,[416] were about as spiritual and soulful as you can possibly get. In Chapter 3 of this opus, "Cemeteries and Shrines," Mumford let's on that humans, like all species, are torn between two poles of being and becoming—that of movement and settlement, with the origin of cities intuitively tied tighter to the latter. Mumford explains while humans are not unique in their urge to settle—e.g., fish and their schools or ants and their anthills or beavers and their colonies—even the earliest human settlements have no animal counterpart: a ceremonious concern for the dead, made real in their concerted burial. Early man's respect for the dead, Mumford argues—while associated with existential anxieties and dread that other species are less capable of—also served a practical purpose: to seek a fixed meeting place and the first permanent settlements. Mumford writes that, "amidst the uneasy wanderings of the paleolithic man, the dead were the first to have a permanent dwelling: a cavern, a mound marked by a cairn, a collective burrow." "In one sense, indeed," Mumford continues, "the city of the dead is the forerunner, almost to the core, of every living city." Mumford called this city of the dead the "Necropolis." [417] Macabre? Nah. Spiritual and Soulful? You bet.

Now, this doesn't mean no work of this sort is being done, or the imbuing of the psyche, soul, and spirit into the thought process of city building. It is only to say not nearly enough of it is. Still, the nascency of what's occurring is useful. In his article called "Understanding the Soul Of A City," [418] Colin Harrison, a technologist and former IBM engineer, takes on the concept, explaining, firstly, of his discussion with a Boeing engineer who told him that airplanes don't really exist but are instead no more than a million parts flying in close formation with not one single part able to fly on its own. "Cities are not designed and engineered like airplanes," Harrison begins, "while individual city blocks, parks, transportation, and so forth are designed and engineered, the city as a whole emerges as patterns of behavior that persist despite the evolution of the natural- and built-environments. Generations of inhabitants organize and interconnect the city's many parts so that it evolves into, not merely a built-environment on top of a natural-environment, but a living entity that we might easily call the 'soul' of the city." [419]

I think of the French word "terroir," which is chiefly used in the context of agriculture that refers to the attributes of a given place, e.g., the geography, geology and climate that, then, interact with a plant's genetics so it's ultimately played out in the quality of select culinary products, including wine, whiskey, and coffee.[420] It is common for terroir to be paired discursively with the phrase "the soul of the land."[421] It is also uncommon, if not unwise, for farmers not to have in the forefront of their mind how terroir creates for a contextual fertility that influences what they grow, why they grow it, and how they grow it.

The concept of terroir, then, is what I am trying arrive at when I tiptoe towards the no man's land that is the psyche, soul, and spirit of the city. Many of the attributes that alchem-

ically combine organically in the creation of a quality product
are also the minerals, mores, and memories that are required
to leaven a lush society. From which sprouts the microenvi-
ronment that is the inclination to invoke the quality of life of a
people which, in turn, is often expressed as a people's ability
to function transcendentally. Or to make meaning in the face
of all that is meaninglessness. As my Shaman put it on a Zoom
call recently, "Without meaning, it is just suffering." A simple
statement, sure. But one that will still knock your socks off if
you marinate on it enough. Echoes Viktor Frankl in his classic
Man's Search for Meaning, "In some ways suffering ceases to be
suffering at the moment it finds a meaning.[422]

I spent a total of four nights and days in the neuro ICU
my second time around. They got my seizure meds in order.
My friends in scrubs— fellow Clevelanders—were rooting for
me to get the hell out of there. Not to lessen the load but because we are in this together. I went jogging down Lakeshore
Blvd., 3 miles, not a month after surgery. No shit. It was late
October but hot. The red, yellow, and orange leaves were falling around me as the bright sun shone. The scene couldn't
have been more sparkling with life before death before afterlife. Cleveland settles into me as I settle ever-closer into Cleveland. But one speck heading back to where I came from. Into
the soul of my city.

And to those I love desperately. You know who you are.
Dance on the toiled soil of me leaving. The only thing in between us is stars. Until they, too, aren't. A god-dead sky stirs
from an agitated finitude. And gets up. A peace of mind
sneaks in the closer to the other side of the equation I get.
Nothing lasts forever. We begrudgingly accept this about hel-

lo, doing so as the salt touches our tongue from the tears that are let go from our eyes. But if that's the case, then why wouldn't it be for goodbye? Meaning, I lean in on the growing intuition that we will meet again. Call it faith. Call it denial. Call it whatever you need to. Do I want to go? Hell no. I fight to stay and watch what's around me flower from love and into love. But I got to go. And so, someday, will you. Like our ancestors did before us. And, God willing, our young will after us. We are a bead of eternity in the fleeting form of 23andMe. And not infrequently, a pearl falls off. I am heading to the promised land with no promises and nothing promised, leaving as I came out: A resilient Rust Belt realist. Yet one finishing what I set out to do. Answering life's question of me, all the while leaving the octopus to be.

Endnotes

1 Raine George "Creating Reagan's image / S.F. ad man Riney helped secure him a second term," San Francisco Chronicle, June 9, 2004, https://www.sfgate.com/business/article/Creating-Reagan-s-image-S-F-ad-man-Riney-2715098.php

2 Michael Beschloss "The Ad That Helped Reagan Sell Good Times to an Uncertain Nation," The New York Times, May 7, 2016. https://www.nytimes.com/2016/05/08/business/the-ad-that-helped-reagan-sell-good-times-to-an-uncertain-nation.html

3 Encyclopedia.com Rust Belt", last modified May 21, 2018. https://www.encyclopedia.com/places/united-states-and-canada/miscellaneous-us-geography/rust-belt

4 "The White House, State of the Union Address", last modified March 1, 2022, https://www.whitehouse.gov/state-of-the-union-2022/

5 Haley BeMiller "Biden touts Intel project in State of the Union," Columbus Dispatch, March 2, 2022, https://www.dispatch.com/story/news/2022/03/01/state-union-biden-tout-ohio-intel-project-address/9330495002/

6 "Ideastream, The Sound of Ideas, 'Rust Belt' Does the Phrase Still Reflect Our Region?", last modified Aug 23, 2016, https://www.ideastream.org/programs/sound-of-ideas/rust-belt-does-the-phrase-still-reflect-our-region

7 Sherrod Brown (@SenSherrodBrown) "You're damn right we're burying the term "Rust Belt," Tweet, March 1, 2022, https://twitter.com/SenSherrodBrown/status/1498853640680976385

8 "Merriam Webster, rust, accessed December 7, 2022 https://www.merriam-webster.com/dictionary/rust

9 Ibid

10 Richard Bienstock, "Scorpions' 'Wind of Change': The Oral History of 1990's Epic Power Ballad," Rolling Stone, September 2, 2015, https://www.rollingstone.com/music/music-news/scorpions-wind-of-change-the-oral-history-of-1990s-epic-power-ballad-63069/

11 "University of Pennsylvania, What is Globalization?", accessed December 7, 2022, https://web.sas.upenn.edu/globalizationstudies/home/globalization-faq/

12 Charles Blow "Them That's Not Shall Lose," The New York Times, July 24, 2011, https://www.nytimes.com/2011/06/25/opinion/25blow.html

13 "Consumer Financial Protection Bureau, What is a payday loan?", last modified Jan 17, 2022, https://www.consumerfinance.gov/ask-cfpb/what-is-a-payday-loan-en-1567/

14 "The Wisdom Portal, Stories of the Human Spirit, T.S. Eliot, The Rock", accessed December 13, 2022, https://www.wisdomportal.com/Technology/TSEliot-TheRock.html

15 Nathan Rousseau, Self, Symbols, and Society, Classic Readings in Social Psychology New York: Rowman & Littlefield Publishers, 2002

16 "Jungian Center for the Spiritual Sciences, Outgrowing the Problems of Life", accessed December 8, 2022, https://jungiancenter.org/outgrowing-the-important-problems-of-life/

17 IBID

18 Carl Gustav Jung, Memories, Dreams, and Reflections New York: Vintage Books Edition, 1989

19 Paul Nelson "Rust Never Sleeps" Rolling Stone, October 18, 1979 https://www.rollingstone.com/music/music-album-reviews/rust-never-sleeps-98395/

20 Richey Piiparinen, "Midnight in America," Belt Magazine, September 23, 2013, https://beltmag.com/midnight-in-the-rust-belt/

21 Eric Holland "Glioblastoma multiforme: the terminator." Proc Natl Acad Sci U S A. 2000 Jun 6;97(12):6242-4, https://doi.org/10.1073/pnas.97.12.6242

22 "American Cancer Society, About Brain and Spinal Cord Tumors in Adults", accessed December 8, 2022, https://www.cancer.org/cancer/brain-spinal-cord-tumors-adults/about.html

23 "National Brain Tumor Society, About Brain Tumors", accessed December 8,2022, https://braintumor.org/

24 Ujjwal Baid "Overall Survival Prediction in Glioblastoma With Radiomic Features Using Machine Learning", Frontiers in Computational Neuroscience, 4 (August 2020) https://doi.org/10.3389/fncom.2020.00061

25 Chaturia Rouse et al "Years of potential life lost for brain and CNS tumors relative to other cancers in adults in the United States, 2010", Neuro-Oncology, 18, Issue 1 (January 2016) https://doi.org/10.1093/neuonc/nov249

26 "National Cancer Institute, Cancer in Children and Adolescents", reviewed November 4, 2021, https://www.cancer.gov/types/childhood-cancers/child-adolescent-cancers-fact-sheet#:~:text=Because%20of%20these%20survival%20improvements,death%20among%20children%20(7).

27 Christopher Hitchens, Mortality New York: Twelve Books, 2012.

28"MedicineNet, Medical Definition of Standard of Care", last reviewed March 29, 2021, https://www.medicinenet.com/standard_of_care/definition.htm

29 Ps.91:5-7 KJV

30 Ps. 23:4-6 KJV

31 Jovi Bon, "Living on a Prayer." Lyrics. Accessed December 29, 2022, https://www.lyrics.com/lyric/2589884/Bon+Jovi/Livin%27+on+a+Prayer

32 Bangles, "Eternal Flame." Genius. Accessed December 29, 2022, https://genius.com/The-bangles-eternal-flame-lyrics

33 Michael Poon et al. "Longer-term (≥ 2 years) survival in patients with glioblastoma in population-based studies pre- and post-2005" Nature, 15, (July 2020) https://www.nature.com/articles/s41598-020-68011-4

34 Alan Wattts, Wisdom for an Age of Insecurity New York: Vintage Books 2011

35 Maria Kli "Eros and Thanatos: A Nondualistic Interpretation: The Dynamic of Drives in Personal and Civilizational Development From Freud to Marcuse", Psychoanalytic Review, 105, 1 (Feb 2018) https://doi.org/10.1521/prev.2018.105.1.67

36 Albert Camus. The Stranger. Translated by Matthew Ward. New York: Vintage Books, 2012

37 "Worldometer's COVID-19 data", accessed December 9, 2022, https://www.worldometers.info/coronavirus/country/us/

38 "Wikipedia, United States Military Casualties of War", last edited on 7 December 2022, https://en.wikipedia.org/wiki/United_States_military_casualties_of_war

39 Nick Judin, "'We Have Forgotten Who We Are': Denial and Death in Mississippi Hospitals" Jackson Free Press, December 9, 2020, https://www.jacksonfreepress.com/news/2020/dec/09/we-have-forgotten-who-we-are-denial-and-death-miss/

40 Derick Thompson, "How Manhattan Became a Rich Ghost Town," The Atlantic, October 15, 2008, https://www.theatlantic.com/ideas/archive/2018/10/new-york-retail-vacancy/572911/

41 U.S. Census Bureau Decennial Census 1900 to 1980, Author's Calculations. "America's Sewage System and the Price of Optimism," Time, August 1, 1969, https://content.time.com/time/subscriber/article/0,33009,901182,00.html

42 Song Meanings, Randy Newman's Burn On" accessed December 10, 2022, https://songmeanings.com/songs/view/37064/

43 Terry Troy, "Cleveland: Reclaiming Its Reputation as the Best Location in

the Nation," Cleveland Magazine, April 19, 2018, https://clevelandmagazine.com/cleader/business/articles/cleveland-reclaiming-its-reputation-as-the-best-location-in-the-nation

44 William S. Dietrich, "A Very Short History of Pittsburgh," Pittsburgh Quarterly, August 25, 2008,

45 Brian Palmer, "How Did Detroit Become Motor City: Why all the big car companies ended up in Michigan," Slate, February, 29, 2012, https://slate.com/news-and-politics/2012/02/why-are-all-the-big-american-car-companies-based-in-michigan.html

46 "University of Virginia, Miller Center, Presidential Speeches," accessed December 10, 2022, https://millercenter.org/the-presidency/presidential-speeches/december-29-1940-fireside-chat-16-arsenal-democracy

47 Arthur Herman, "Business Skills Saved the U.S. at the Dawn of World War II," Daily Beast, July 13, 2017, https://www.thedailybeast.com/bill-knudsens-business-skills-saved-the-us-at-the-dawn-of-world-war-ii#:~:text=Bill%20Knudsen%20was%20president%20of,America%20but%20the%20free%20world.

48 "University of Virginia, Miller Center, Presidential Speeches," accessed December 10, 2022, https://millercenter.org/the-presidency/presidential-speeches/december-29-1940-fireside-chat-16-arsenal-democracy

49 Kat Eschner, How Detroit Went from Motor City to the Arsenal of Democracy," Smithsonian Magazine, March 28, 2017, https://www.smithsonianmag.com/smart-news/when-detroit-was-arsenal-democracy-180962620/

50 Brian Albrecht, James Banks, Cleveland in World War II Charleston: The History Press, 2015

51 IBID

52 IBID

53 Andrew Shonfield, Modern Capitalism, Oxford: Oxford University Press, 1969

54 Stephen Dubner "Detroit is Dying… Quickly," Freakonomics, March 23, 2011, https://freakonomics.com/2011/03/detroit-is-dying-quickly/

55 U.S. Bureau of Economic Analysis, "CAINC4 Personal income and employment by major component" (accessed Monday, January 9, 2023).

56 John Skow, "Can Cleveland escape burning?" The Saturday Evening Post, July 29 1967, https://www.unz.com/print/SatEveningPost-7jul29-00038/

57 IBID

58 https://pressbooks.ulib.csuohio.edu/plain-dealing/chapter/roldo-barti-mole-cleveland-newspapers-1965/ 22222222, RB

59 "The Cleveland Memory Project, The d. a. levy collection", accessed December 10, 2022, http://www.clevelandmemory.org/levy/bio.html

60 IBID

61 David Stradling, Richard Stradling, "Perceptions of the Burning River: Deindustrialization and Cleveland's Cuyahoga River," Environmental History, No. 3 (Jul., 2008): 515-535 13, https://www.jstor.org/stable/25473265

62 Author's Calculations, Decennial Census

63 Daniel Kerr "Who Burned Cleveland, Ohio? The Forgotten Fires of the 1970s" in Flammable Cities: Fire, Urban Environment, and Culture in History, ed. Jordan Sand, Greg Bankoff, and Uwe Luebken Madison: University of Wisconsin Press, 2012),

64 IBID

65 Edward Whelan, "The Bombing Business," Cleveland Magazine, February 15, 2017, https://clevelandmagazine.com/entertainment/film-tv/articles/the-bombing-business

66 IBID

67 Brent Larkin, "Forty years ago, Cleveland became the first major U.S. city since the Depression to fall into default. Here's how it happened," Cleveland Plain Dealer, December 2016, 2018, https://www.cleveland.com/opinion/2018/12/forty-years-ago-cleveland-became-the-first-major-us-city-since-the-depression-to-fall-into-default-heres-how-it-happened-brent-larkin.html

68 Gene Kosowan, "Why Cleveland Is Often Called 'The Mistake on The Lake,'" The Travel, May 28, 2022, https://www.thetravel.com/why-is-cleveland-the-mistake-on-the-lake/

69 Albin Krebs "An Apology to Cleveland", February 26, 1981, https://www.nytimes.com/1981/02/26/nyregion/notes-on-people-an-apology-to-cleveland.html

70 Yakov Smirnoff (@Yakov_Smirnoff) "In every country, they make fun of city. In U.S. you make fun of Cleveland. In Russia, we make fun of Cleveland", Tweet, August, 13, 2015, https://twitter.com/Yakov_Smirnoff/status/631864133739225090

71 Gene Kosowan, "Why Cleveland Is Often Called 'The Mistake On The Lake'", The Travel, May 28, 2022, https://www.thetravel.com/why-is-cleveland-the-mistake-on-the-lake/

72 "Simply Psychology, Psychodynamic Approach/ Freud/Defense Mechanisms", last reviewed 2020,https://www.simplypsychology. org/d,efense-mechanisms.html

73 Andy Horowitz, "Hurricane Katrina Showed Us How Spectacularly the Government Can Fail Its People. Fifteen Years Later, the Pattern Continues," Time August, 26, 2020, https://time.com/5883614/hurricane-katrina-corona-virus/

74 Joe Walders, "The Man Who Made Cleveland a National Joke", Cleveland Magazine, January 1, 1976, https://clevelandmagazine.com/in-the-cle/ the-read/articles/the-man-who-made-cleveland-a-national-joke

75 Christine Jindra, "From a comic career to a tragic life Emmy-winning writer now homeless in his native Cleveland", Cleveland Plain Dealer, March, 27, 2008, https://www.cleveland.com/pdextra/2008/04/from_a_com-ic_career_to_a_tragi.html

76 cseper,"Jack Hanrahan dead at 75," Cleveland Plain Dealer, April 28, 2008, https://www.cleveland.com/metro/2008/04/jack_hanrahan_dead_at_75.html

77 Herman Melville, Moby-Dick; or, The Whale, New York: Harper & Brothers, 1851

78 "Society of Analytical Psychology, Jungian Psychology, The Jungian Shadow", last updated August12, 2015, https://www.thesap.org.uk/ articles-on-jungian-psychology-2/about-analysis-and-therapy/the-shadow/

79 "Demographia, Largest US Cities: 1950," accessed December 16, 2022, http://demographia.com/db-uscityr1950.htm

80 Peter Drucker, "The New Society of Organizations", Harvard Business Review, September-October, 1992, https://hbr.org/1992/09/the-new-society-of-organizations

81 "Cleveland overtakes Detroit as poorest big city in U.S., census finds," The Detroit News, September 17, 2020, https://www.detroitnews.com/story/ news/local/detroit-city/2020/09/17/cleveland-overtakes-detroit-poorest-big-city-u-s-census/

82 "Ed Glaeser, "Reinventing Boston: 1640-2003", Harvard Institute of Economic Research, Discussion Paper Number 2017, September, 2003, https://scholar.harvard.edu/files/glaeser/files/reinventing_boston_1640-2003. pdf

83 "Laura Klappenbach, "Descent with Modification", Thought Co., January 16, 2019, https://www.thoughtco.com/descent-with-modification-129878

84 IBID

85 Joseph Schumpeter, Capitalism, Socialism, and Democracy, New York: Harper & Brothers, 1942

86 The Nobel Prize, Simon Kuznets Prize Lecture," accessed December 12, 2022, https://www.nobelprize.org/prizes/economic-sciences/1971/kuznets/lecture/

87 Chris Briem, "Clairton is Dead Long Live Clairton," Pittsburgh Post-Gazette, June 6, 2021, https://www.post-gazette.com/opinion/Op-Ed/2021/06/06/As-others-see-it-Clairton-is-dead-long-live-Clairton-Christopher-Briem/stories/202106020011

88 Cimino, Michael. The Deer Hunter (DMI, 1978), 3 hour 3 minutes. https://dvd.netflix.com/Movie/The-Deer-Hunter/431994

89 Michael McIntyre, "Clevelanders probably think they don't have an accent, but we do, and so do others in the Midwest," Cleveland Plain Dealer, January, 13, 2017, https://www.cleveland.com/tipoff/2017/01/clevelanders_probably_think_th.html

90 Jill Desmini, "Wild Innovation: Stoss In Detroit", Scenario Journal, Spring 2013, https://scenariojournal.com/article/wild-innovation/

91 "Stanford Encyclopedia of Philosophy, Heraclitus, last revision, September 3, 2019, https://plato.stanford.edu/entries/heraclitus/

92 James Risen, "Assembly Line Flexibility Sets Japanese Apart", Los Angeles Times, January 14, 1990, https://www.latimes.com/archives/la-xpm-1990-01-14-fi-393-story.html

93 Joseph Schumpeter, Capitalism, Socialism, and Democracy, New York: Harper & Brothers, 1942

94 "Oxford Reference, disinformation", accessed December 12, 2022, https://www.oxfordreference.com/view/10.1093/oi/authority.20110803095721660

95 Sara Brown, "What Microsoft's Satya Nadella thinks about work of the future," MIT School of Management Ideas Made to Matter, November 24, 2020, https://mitsloan.mit.edu/ideas-made-to-matter/what-microsofts-satya-nadella-thinks-about-work-future

96 Eric Weiner, "The 19th-Century Philosopher Who Predicted Data Overload," Medium, blog post, June 29, 2021, https://ericweiner.medium.com/the-19th-century-philosopher-who-predicted-data-overload-67eee-2af7497

97 Craig S. Smith "A.I. Here, There, Everywhere," New York Times, February 23,2021, https://www.nytimes.com/2021/02/23/technology/ai-innovation-privacy-seniors-education.html

98 Robert Ginsberg, The Aesthetics of Ruins, Amsterdam: Rodopi, 2004

99 Tom Leonard, "US cities may have to be bulldozed in order to survive," The Telegraph, June 12,2009, https://www.telegraph.co.uk/finance/financialcrisis/5516536/US-cities-may-have-to-be-bulldozed-in-order-to-survive.html

100 Richey Piiparinen, "Rust Belt Fatalism: Why Psychology is Important in City Making," Huffington Post, July 18,2012, https://www.huffpost.com/entry/post_b_1680129

101 "Lincoln Institute of Land Policy, Publications, Policy Focus Reports, 'Regenerating America's Legacy Cities'," May 2013, https://www.lincolninst.edu/publications/policy-focus-reports/regenerating-americas-legacy-cities

102 IBID

103 Nietzsche, Friedrich Wilhelm. The Gay Science (the Joyful Wisdom). United States: DIGIREADS.COM, 2009.

104 "WebMD, Mental Health, Reference, What is Scarcity Mentality?" https://www.webmd.com/mental-health/what-is-scarcity-mentality

105 Michael Chapman, All the Right Moves (20th Century Fox,1983), 1 hour 31minutes.https://www.netflixmovies.com/all-the-right-moves-1983

106 Cade Metz, "Jay Last, One of the Rebels Who Founded Silicon Valley, Dies at 92," New York Times, November 20 2021, https://www.nytimes.com/2021/11/20/technology/jay-last-dead.html

107 Arthur Koestler, The Ghost and the Machine, London:Hutchinson, 1967

108 Gerald Svensden, "Population Parameters and Colony Composition of Beaver (Castor canadensis) in Southeast Ohio," The American Midland Naturalist, 104, no.1 (July 1980):47-56, https://www.jstor.org/stable/2424957

109 Matt Phillips, "Too Big to Fail: The Entire Private Sector," The New York Times, May 19,2020, https://www.nytimes.com/2020/05/19/business/too-big-to-fail-wall-street-businesses.html?smid=url-share

110 "International Monetary Fund, IMF Working Papers, How Well Do Economists Forecast Recessions?", March 5, 2008, https://www.imf.org/en/Publications/WP/Issues/2018/03/05/How-Well-Do-Economists-Forecast-Recessions-45672

111 IBID

112 Chris Hamby, "Behind the Scenes, McKinsey Guided Companies at the Center of the Opioid Crisis," June 29,2022, https://www.nytimes.com/2022/06/29/business/mckinsey-opioid-crisis-opana.html?smid=url-share

113 "Joint Economic Committee, Chairman Don Beyer, "The Economic Toll of the Opioid Crisis Reached Nearly $1.5 Trillion in 2020," accessed December 30, 2022, https://www.jec.senate.gov/public/_cache/files/67bced7f-4232-40ea-9263-f033d280c567/jec-cost-of-opioids-issue-brief.pdf

114 "The Decision Lab, Homo Economicus," accessed December 16,2022, https://thedecisionlab.com/reference-guide/economics/homo-economicus

115 Marion Fourcade, "The Superiority of Economists," Journal of Economic Perspectives 29, no. 1 (Winter 2015):89-214, https://pubs.aeaweb.org/doi/pdf/10.1257/jep.29.1.89

116 Rev 3:16-17 KJV.

117 Robert J. Shiller, "Narrative Economics," American Economic Review, 107, no. 4 (April 2017):967-1004, DOI: 10.1257/aer.107.4.967

118 IBID

119 Joel Mokyr, "Cultural entrepreneurs and the origins of modern economic growth," Scandinavian Economic History Review 61, issue 1 (March 2003): 1-33, https://doi.org/10.1080/03585522.2012.755471

120 Milton Friedman, "A Friedman doctrine-- The Social Responsibility Of Business Is to Increase Its Profits," The New York Times September 13, 1970, https://www.nytimes.com/1970/09/13/archives/a-friedman-doctrine-the-social-responsibility-of-business-is-to.html

121 Amos Tversky and Daniel Kahneman, "Rational Choice and the Framing of Decisions," The Behavioral Foundations of Economic Theory, 59, no.4 (October 1986): 251-278, https://www.jstor.org/stable/i340501

122 Richard Shiller, Narrative Economics, Princeton, NJ: Princeton University Press,2019

123 IBID

124 "Margaret Thatcher: a life in quotes," The Guardian April 8, 2020, https://www.theguardian.com/politics/2013/apr/08/margaret-thatcher-quotes

125 Gerald Epstein, "Financialization, Rentier Interests, and Central Bank Policy," Paper prepared for PERI Conference on "Financialization of the World Economy", December 7-8,2001, https://peri.umass.edu/fileadmin/pdf/financial/fin_Epstein.pdf

126 "World Inequality Database, Country, USA, accessed December 18 2022, https://wid.world/country/usa/

127 Rachel Nuwer, "How Conversations Around Campfire Might Have Shaped Human Cognition And Culture," Smithsonian Magazine, Septem-

ber,22, 2014, https://www.smithsonianmag.com/smart-news/late-night-conversations-around-fire-might-have-shaped-early-human-cognition-and-culture-180952790/#.Y7Ye1p1PHvA.link

128 Jeffrey Pfeffer, Managing with power, Boston: Harvard University Press,1992

129 Steven Woolf, Heidi Shoomaker, "Life Expectancy and Mortality Rates in the United States, 1959-2017," JAMA 322,20 (November 26 2019): 1996-2016, https://doi.org/10.1001/jama.2019.16932

130 Mary Kate Brogan," Working-age Americans dying at higher rates, especially in economically hard-hit states," VCU News, November 26,2019, https://news.vcu.edu/article/workingage_americans_dying_at_higher_rates_especially_in_economically

131 "Worldometer's COVID-19 data", last edited December 15, 2022, https://www.worldometers.info/coronavirus/#countries

132 Roger Martin, "Efficient Companies Made the United States Weak," The Washington Post March 27,2020, https://www.washingtonpost.com/outlook/2020/03/27/economic-efficiency-resilience-coronavirus/

133 OECD (2023), Life expectancy at birth (indicator). doi: 10.1787/27e0fc9d-en, Accessed January, 5, 2023,

134 "Wikipedia, Gigli saw," last edited June 2, 2022, https://en.wikipedia.org/wiki/Gigli_saw

135 James Goodrich, "How to get in and out of the skull: from tumi to 'hammer and chisel' to the Gigli saw and the osteoplastic flap," Journal of Neurosurgery 36, issue 4, https://doi.org/10.3171/2014.2.FOCUS13543

136 "Cleveland State University, Maxine Levin College of Urban Affairs, Center for Population Dynamics, Reports and Blogs, Press and Expert Commentary," accessed January, 15, 2023, https://levin.urban.csuohio.edu/cpd/reports_blogs.html#press_expert

137 CBC News, "In the Shadow of Steel: Hamilton and the search for a new future," September 12,2013, https://www.cbc.ca/news/canada/hamilton/headlines/in-the-shadow-of-steel-hamilton-and-the-search-for-a-new-future-1.1701443

138 Sam Keen, "The heroics of everyday life: A theorist of death confronts his own end," Psychology Today, April 1974, https://oxfordexperience2017.files.wordpress.com/2014/07/keen-becker-interview.pdf

139 Ernest Becker, The Denial of Death, New York: Free Press, 1973

140 Adam Adamski, "Archetypes and the Collective Unconscious of Carl G. Jung in the Light of Quantum Psychology," Neuro Quantology, 9, issue 3

(September 2011) 563–571, https://www.neuroquantology.com/data-cms/articles/20191024063924pm413.pdf

141 R.G.L. Waite "Adolf Hitler's Guilt Feelings: A Problem in History and Psychology," The Journal of Interdisciplinary History 1, no. 2 (Winter, 1971) 229-249, https://doi.org/10.2307/202642

142 Pawnbroker, directed by Sidney Lumet (American International Pictures,1965). 1 hour, 46 minutes. https://www.imdb.com/title/tt0059575/

143 Sam Keen, "The heroics of everyday life: A theorist of death confronts his own end," Psychology Today, April 1974, https://oxfordexperience2017.files.wordpress.com/2014/07/keen-becker-interview.pdf

144 L. Linn Mackey "The Collective Unconscious and the Akashic Field," Jung Journal: Culture & Psyche 1, no.2 (Spring 2007) 2-15, https://doi.org/10.1525/jung.2007.1.2.2

145 Susan Sontag, Illness as Metaphor, New York: Farrar, Straus and Giroux, 1978

146 IBID

147 Richey Piiparinen, "Improving health care for the people will change Cleveland, and the world," Cleveland Plain Dealer, September 13, 2020, https://www.cleveland.com/opinion/2020/09/improving-health-care-for-the-people-will-change-cleveland-and-the-world-richey-piiparinen.html

148 Richey Piiparinen, "Use Rescue Plan Act dollars to rescue Cleveland's health," Cleveland Plain Dealer, October 27,2021, https://www.cleveland.com/opinion/2021/10/use-rescue-plan-act-dollars-to-rescue-clevelands-health-richey-piiparinen.html

149 Tom Mihaljevic and Cliff A. Megerian, "Cleveland Clinic-UH collaboration expanding beyond COVID-19," Cleveland Plain Dealer September 13, 2020, https://www.cleveland.com/opinion/2020/09/cleveland-clinic-uh-collaboration-expanding-beyond-covid-19-tom-mihaljevic-and-cliff-a-megerian.html

150 Richey Piiparinen and Joshua Valdez, "Swimming Upstream: Getting to the Root Causes of Infant Mortality and Life Expectancy Outcomes in Cleveland, Ohio and the U.S." Urban Publications (October 2021), https://engagedscholarship.csuohio.edu/urban_facpub/1748

151 OECD (2023), Health spending (indicator). doi: 10.1787/8643de7e-en (Accessed on 07 January 2023)

152 "History of Medicine Division, National Library of Medicine, National Institutes of Health, Greek Medicine," last updated, February, 72012, https://www.nlm.nih.gov/hmd/greek/greek_hippocrates.html

153 Austin Frakt, Reagan, "Deregulation and America's Exceptional Rise in Health Care Costs, "The New York Times, June 4, 2018, https://www.nytimes.com/2018/06/04/upshot/reagan-deregulation-and-americas-exceptional-rise-in-health-care-costs.html

154 IBID

155 Sam Keen, "The heroics of everyday life: A theorist of death confronts his own end," Psychology Today, April 1974, https://oxfordexperience2017.files.wordpress.com/2014/07/keen-becker-interview.pdf

156 Sam Keen, "The heroics of everyday life: A theorist of death confronts his own end," Psychology Today, April 1974, https://oxfordexperience2017.files.wordpress.com/2014/07/keen-becker-interview.pdf

157 "Russian Poetry.Net, G.R. Derzhavin, Бог/God," http://max.mmlc.northwestern.edu/mdenner/Demo/texts/god.htm

158 Paula Braveman and Laura Gottleib, "The Social Determinants of Health: It's Time to Consider the Causes of the Causes," Public Health Reports, 129 suppl. 2 (Jan-Feb 2014) 19-31, doi: 10.1177/00333549141291S206

159 David Brancaccio, "A way to save both lives and the economy during the COVID-19 pandemic," Marketplace, March 26, 2020, https://www.marketplace.org/2020/03/26/covid-19-economy-testing-masks/

160 George Akerloff and Robert J. Shiller, Animal Spirits: How Human Psychology Drives the Economy, and Why It Matters for Global Capitalism,, Princeton: Princeton University Press,2009

161 IBID

162 Manuel Albers, "Do Maps Make Geography? Part 1: Redlining, Planned Shrinkage, and the Places of Decline," ACME: An International E-Journal for Critical Geographies 13, no. 4 (2014):525-556, https://acme-journal.org/index.php/acme/article/view/1036

163 Ed Glaeser, "Can Buffalo Ever Come Back?," City Journal, Autumn, 2007, https://www.city-journal.org/html/can-buffalo-ever-come-back-13050.html

164 IBID

165 Gunmar Branson, "Tightening the Belts: Rethinking Sun vs. Rust," Summit Journal, March 25, 2021, https://www.afire.org/summit/sunvsrust/#notes

166 Siobahn Lyons, "Psychogeography: a way to delve into the soul of a city," Conversation, June 2018, 2017, https://theconversation.com/psychogeography-a-way-to-delve-into-the-soul-of-a-city-78032

167 Philip Roth, Zuckerman Bound, New York: Farrar, Straus, and Giroux, 1965

168 John F. Kennedy, "New England and the South," The Atlantic, January, 1954, https://www.theatlantic.com/magazine/archive/1954/01/new-england-and-the-south/376244/

169 IBID

170 Francis Ysidro Edgeworth, Mathematical Psychics: An Essay on the Application of Mathematics to the Moral Sciences, London C. Kegan Paul and Co., 1881

171 Bob Strauss, "How the "Invisible Hand" of the Market Does, and Does Not, Work," ThoughtCo., February 28,2018, https://www.thoughtco.com/invisible-hand-definition-4147674

172 Adam Smith, An Inquiry into the Nature and Causes of the Wealth of Nations, London: Methuen and Co., Ltd., 1904

173 Phill.2:4 BSB

174 Warren Samuels, Erasing the Invisible Hand: Essays on an Elusive and Misused Concept in Economics, Boston: Cambridge University Press, 2011

175 Laura Pennacchi, "Does it make sense to question the morality of capitalism?" Social Europe, April 19,2021, https://www.socialeurope.eu/does-it-make-sense-to-question-the-morality-of-capitalism

176 Amartya Sen, "Rational Fools: A Critique of the Behavioral Foundations of Economic Theory," Philosophy & Public Affairs, 6, no. 4 (Summer, 1977): 317-344, http://www.jstor.org/stable/2264946

177 "Meaning In, Quotes, John D Rockefeller, accessed December 31, 2022, https://meaningin.com/quotes/john-d---rockefeller/40962-i-have-ways-of-making-money-that-you-know-nothing-

178 Dalia Marin and Thierry Verdier, "Power inside the Firm and the Market: A General Equilibrium Approach," Journal of European Economic Association,6, no.4 (June 2008):752-788, https://www.jstor.org/stable/40282683

179 Simeon Alder et al. "The Decline of the U.S. Rust Belt: A Macroeconomic Analysis," Center for Quantitative Economic Research Working Paper Series, Working paper 14-05 (August 2014), https://www.atlantafed.org/-/media/documents/cqer/publications/workingpapers/cqer_wp1405

180 IBID

181 Godfellas directed by Martin Scorcese (Warner Brothers, 1990) 2 hours

and 25 minutes, https://www.imdb.com/title/tt0099685/

182 Alexis de Tocqueville, Democracy in America, London: Saunders and Otley, 1835-1840

183 Sheldon Solomon et al, Worm at the Core: On the Role of Death in Life, New York: Random House, 2015

184 Alexis de Tocqueville, Democracy in America, London: Saunders and Otley, 1835-1840

185 "Leave it to Beaver Transcripts," accessed December 21, 2022, https://virtualtrials.org/dcvax.cfm

186 William Schneider, "The Suburban Century Begins," The Atlantic, July, 1992, https://www.theatlantic.com/past/docs/politics/ecbig/schnsub.htm

187 Ernest Becker, The Denial of Death, New York: Free Press, 1973

188 Pete Beatty, "Train Dreams, Part 1," Belt Magazine December 16 2003, https://beltmag.com/train-dreams-part-1/

189 William Schneider, The Suburban Century Begins," The Atlantic Monthly, July 1992, https://www.theatlantic.com/past/docs/politics/ecbig/schnsub.htm

190 Alan Horwitz, "How an Age of Anxiety Became an Age of Depression," Milbank Quarterly,88,1 (March 88):112-138, https://doi.org/10.1111/j.1468-0009.2010.00591.x

191 Hanson Baldwin, "The Atomic Weapon," The New York Times, August 7, 1945, 10 https://timesmachine.nytimes.com/timesmachine/1945/08/07/88273715.html?pageNumber=10

192 K Tobin, "The Reduction of Urban Vulnerability: Revisiting 1950s American Suburbanization as Civil Defence," War History, 2, 2 (September 2002):1-32, https://doi.org/10.1080/713999949.

193 Marschak, E. Teller, and L R. Klein, "Dispersal of Cities and Industries," Bulletin of Atomic Scientists 1, no.9 (1946): 13-15,20

194 Robert Neinlein, "The Last Days of the United States," in Expanded Universe, New York: Ace Books, 1980

195 Fred Charles Iklé, Social Impact of Bomb Destruction, Norman,OK: University of Oklahoma Press, 1958

196 Ralph Lapp, Must We Hide? New York: Addison-Wesley Press, 1949

197 IBID

198 "Mobilization of the National Economy in the Face of Atomic Attack," Oral Presentations (Washington, DC: Industrial College of the Armed Forces, 1953-1954), p.22.

199 US Congress, The Joint Committee on the Economic Report, The Need For Industrial Dispersal, Report by the Staff of the Joint Committee on the Economic Report, 82nd Congress, 1st Session (Washington: US Government Printing Office, 1951), 56 pp., https://www.jec.senate.gov/reports/82nd%20 Congress/The%20Need%20for%20Industrial%20Dispersal%20(44).pdf

200 IBID

201 Clifford Edward Clark, The American Family Home, 1800-1960, Chapel Hill: University of North Carolina Press, 1986

202 Leo F. Schnore, "The Growth of Metropolitan Suburbs," American Sociological Review 22, no.2 (April 1957):.l65-173, https://doi.org/10.2307/2088853
203 Ralph Lapp, Must We Hide? New York: Addison-Wesley Press, 1949

204 Tracy B. Augur, "Dispersal is Good Business," Bulletin of Atomic Scientists, 6, issue9 (SeptOctober (1948):244-245, https://doi.org/10.1080/0096 3402.1950.11461278

205 Tobin, "The Reduction of Urban Vulnerability: Revisiting 1950s American Suburbanization as Civil Defence," War History, 2, 2 (September 2002):1-32, https://doi.org/10.1080/713999949

206 IBID

207 IBID

208 Katherine Rye Jewell, Dollars for Dixie, Boston: Cambridge University Press,2017

209 Farhad Manjoo, ""It's the End of California as We Know It," The New York Times, October 30, 1019, https://www.nytimes.com/2019/10/30/ opinion/sunday/california-fires.html

210 Gunmar Branson, "Tightening the Belts: Rethinking Sun vs. Rust," Summit Journal, March 25, 2021, https://www.afire.org/summit/ sunvsrust/#notes

211 Hans Johnson, "Who's Leaving California—and Who's Moving In?" Public Policy Institute Of California Blog, March 28, 2022, https://www.ppic.org/blog/whos-leaving-california-and-whos-moving-in/

212 "Nothing Rotten about the Big Plum," Time, June 15,1981, https:// content.time.com/time/subscriber/article/0,33009,949179,00.html

213 Dan Fitzpatrick, "Region is portrayed as a 'cool' place to live," Pittsburgh Post-Gazette, December 19,2000, https://old.post-gazette.com/bus inessnews/20001219luringside4.asp

214 Rich Piiparinen and Jon Smith, "Stress Symptoms of Two Groups before and after the Terrorist Attacks of 9/11/01," Perceptual and Motor Skills,97,issue2(August 2016), https://doi.org/10.2466/pms.2003.97.2.360

215 Chekhov, Anton Pavlovich. Swan Song. Czechia: Good Press, 2019.

216 Nick Tabor "No Slouch," Paris Review, April 7, 2015, https://www. theparisreview.org/blog/2015/04/07/no-slouch/

217 Emile Durkheim, Division of Labor and Society, Translation, W.D. Walls, New York: Free Press,1997

218 2016 https://www.cleveland.com/opinion/2016/09/clevelands_come-back_has_to_be.html

219 Gen 3:13 ESV.

220 Carolyn Gregoire, "The Unexpected Reason It's Healthy To Feel Shame," Huffington Post, March 3, 2016, https://www.huffpost.com/entry/shame-psychology-evolution_n_56d4428ce4b0871f60ebf5c9

221 Saint-Exupéry, Antoine de. The Little Prince. London: Wordsworth Editions Limited, 2021.

222 Zuk-Nae Lee, "Korean Culture and the Sense of Shame," Transcultural Psychiatry, 36, issue 2 (June, 2016):181-194, https://doi.org/10.1177/136346159903600202

223 Charles Cooley, Human Nature and the Social Order, New York: Scribner's, 1922.

224 Tara Isabella Burton, "The Geography of Melancholy," The American Reader 2015, https://theamericanreader.com/the-geography-of-melancholy/

225 Evan Andrews, "What is Seppuku", History, August 22, 2018, https://www.history.com/news/what-is-seppuku

226 Richey Piiparinen, "Why "Rust Belt" Is Not A Pejorative," Belt Magazine, August 18,2013, https://beltmag.com/why-rust-belt-is-not-a-pejo-rative/

227 Annagret Haase et al, "Representing urban shrinkage — The impor-tance of discourse as a frame for understanding conditions and policy," Cities, 69 (September 2017): 95-101, https://doi.org/10.1016/j.cit-ies.2016.09.007

228 Richey Piiparinen, "In Defense of Ruin Porn," Next City, February 7, 2012, https://nextcity.org/urbanist-news/in-defense-of-ruin-porn

229 Arthur Chu, "Cleveland Comes Crawling Back to LeBron: The Masochism of Rust Belt Chic," Daily Beast, July 12, 2007, https://www.thedaily-beast.com/cleveland-comes-crawling-back-to-lebron-the-masochism-of-rust-belt-chic

230 IBID

231 Steven Greenhouse, "A kick in the stomach': massive GM layoffs leave workers distraught – and angry", The Guardian, December 27,2018, https://www.theguardian.com/business/2018/dec/27/general-motors-ohio-auto-car-layoffs

232 IBID

233 Thomas Scheff "Shame and the Social Bond:A Sociological Theory," Sociological Theory, 18, issue (June 21,2016): tps://doi.org/10.1111/0735-2751.0008

234 Benjamin Wallace-Wells, "Donald Trump and The Idea of the Rust Belt," The New Yorker, June 1, 2016, https://www.newyorker.com/news/benjamin-wallace-wells/donald-trump-and-the-idea-of-the-rust-belt

235 IBID

236 IBID

237 Michelle Cottle, "The 'Disney' for Boomers Puts Hedonism on Full Display," The New York Times, March, 3, 2022, https://www.nytimes.com/2022/03/03/opinion/florida-the-villages.html

238 Chila Woychik, On Being a Rat and Other Observations, Shellsburg IA: Port Yonder Press, 2012.

239 Sigmund Freud, The Complete Psychological Works of Sigmund Freud, London: Hogarth Press, 1955

240 Cimino, Michael. The Deer Hunter (DMI, 1978), 3 hour 3 minutes. https://dvd.netflix.com/Movie/The-Deer-Hunter/431994

241 Bigelow, Kathryn, The Hurt Locker (Voltage Pictures, 2009), 2 hour, 3 minutes. https://www.imdb.com/title/tt0887912/

242 Coppola Francis Ford, Apocalypse Now (American Zoetrope,1979) 2 hour, 27 minutes. https://www.imdb.com/title/tt0078788/

243 Christine Baker, Feemale Survivors of Sexual Abuse: An Integrated Guide to Treatment, London: Brunner-Routledge, 2002

244 April Zeoli et al, "Homicide as Infectious Disease: Using Public Health Methods to Investigate the Diffusion of Homicide," Justice Quarterly,31, no.3 (2014):609-632, . https://doi.org/10.1080/07418825.2012.732100.

245 Herbert Silberer, Alchemy and Psychoanalysis, New York: The Lost Library, 2016.

246 Resmaa Menakem, My Grandmother's Hands Racialized Trauma and the Pathway to Mending Our Hearts and Bodies, London: Penguin Books Limited, 2017

247 James Baldwin, The Fire Next Time, New York: Dial Press, 1963

248 James Baldwin, The Evidence of Things Not Seen, New York: Holt, Rinehart, and Winston, 1985

249 James K. Rowe, "Baldwin and Buddhism: Death Denial, White Supremacy, and the Promise of Racial Justice," The Arrow, December, 16, 2020, https://arrow-journal.org/baldwin-and-buddhism-death-denial-white-supremacy-and-the-promise-of-racial-justice/

250 Angus Deaton and Anne Case, Deaths of Despair and the Future of Capitalism, Princeton, NJ: Princeton University Press, 2021.

251 Spencer Lee-Lenfield, "Anatomists of Melancholy in the Age of Coronavirus," The Chronicle, April 17,2020, https://www.chronicle.com/article/anatomists-of-melancholy-in-the-age-of-coronavirus/

252 Alex Ross, "Nietzsche's Eternal Return," The New Yorker, October, 7, 2019, https://www.newyorker.com/magazine/2019/10/14/nietzsches-eternal-return

253 Zoe Williams, "Trauma, trust, and triumph: Psychiatrist Bessel van der Kolk on how to recover from our deepest pain," The Guardian, September 20, 2021, https://www.theguardian.com/society/2021/sep/20/trauma-trust-and-triumph-psychiatrist-bessel-van-der-kolk-on-how-to-recover-from-our-deepest-pain

254 Nietzsche, Friedrich Wilhelm. The Joyful Wisdom. United Kingdom: T. N. Foulis, 1910.

255 Bernardo Kastrup, "Modern Tales of the Dioscuri: The Quest for Truth," Metaphysical Speculations, Bernardo Kastrup's medications on life and the universe, February 10, 2013, https://www.bernardokastrup.com/2013/02/

256 Richard Dawkins, River out of Eden: A Darwinian View of Life, New York: Basic Books,1996

257 Al Fernandez, "Understanding Faith,: The Harvard Crimson, October 17, 2004, https://www.thecrimson.com/column/row-the-boat/article/2014/10/17/understanding-faith-secular-age/#.Y6YRXYPr2v4.link

258 Ezra Klein, "This Conversation Will Change How You Think About Trauma." The New York Times, August 24, 2021, https://www.nytimes.com/2021/08/24/opinion/ezra-klein-podcast-van-der-kolk.html?showTranscript=1

259 Bessel van der Kolk, The Body Keeps the Score: Brain, Mind, and Body in the Healing of Trauma, New York: Viking Press, 2014

260 Ezra Klein, "This Conversation Will Change How You Think About Trauma." The New York Times, August 24, 2021, https://www.nytimes.com/2021/08/24/opinion/ezra-klein-podcast-van-der-kolk.html?showTranscript=1

261 IBID

262 J Becker and G.A.DaSilva, "Speechless soma: The trauma's language in the psychosomatic," European Psychiatry, 33 (March 2016):388, https://doi.org/10.1016/j.eurpsy.2016.01.1395

263 IBID

264 Carl Gustav Jung, Synchronicity: An Acausal Connecting Principle Translated by R.F.C. Hull, Princeton, NJ: Princeton University Press, 1973.

265 "Donnelly Center, News, Brain Cancer Linked to Tissue Healing," last updated January 4, 2021,https://thedonnellycentre.utoronto.ca/news/brain-cancer-linked-tissue-healing

266 Pat Galbincea, "Coroner rules that Harvey Pekar's death due to 'natural causes'," The Cleveland Plain Dealer. October 19,2010, https://www.cleveland.com/metro/2010/10/coroner_rules_that_harvey_peka.html#:~:text=%22His%20death%20came%20as%20a,seizure%20threshold%20when%20used%20incorrectly.

267 IBID

268 "American History from Revolution to Reconstruction, 1860-1914, Midwestern Realism,", http://www.let.rug.nl/usa/outlines/literature-1991/the-rise-of-realism-1860-1914/midwestern-realism.php

269 Hellen Thomas Follet, "Contemporary Novelists: William Dean Howells," The Atlantic, March 1917, https://www.theatlantic.com/magazine/archive/1917/03/contemporary-novelists-william-dean-howells/304476/

270 IBID

271 Mark Mullen, "The Gentle Art?" Jiu Jitsu Times, August 25, 2017, https://jiujitsutimes.com/the-gentle-art/

272 Mona Chalabi, "What Are The Demographics Of Heaven?"

FiveThirtyEight,October 14,2015, https://fivethirtyeight.com/features/
what-are-the-demographics-of-heaven/

273 IBID

274 Joseph Bottum "All That Lives Must Die," First Things, May, 1996,
https://www.firstthings.com/article/1996/05/all-that-lives-must-die

275 This Day in Quotes, 'nothing is certain except death and taxes."
November 2013, 2010, accessed 12/23/2022, http://www.thisdayinquotes.
com/2010/11/nothing-is-certain-except-death-and.html

276 Maria Popova, "How to Live to the Full While Dying: The Extraordi-
nary Diary of Alice James, William and Henry James's Brilliant Sister," The
Marginalian, August 7,, 2017,https://www.themarginalian.org/2017/08/07/
diary-of-alice-james-death/

277"Open Source Shakespeare, Plays, Tragedy of Julius Caesar, Act II, Scene
2," accessed January, 25, 2023 https://www.opensourceshakespeare.org/
views/plays/play_view.php?WorkID=juliuscaesar&Act=2

278 Paul Kalanithi, "How Long Have I Got Left?" The New York Times,
January 24, 2014, https://www.nytimes.com/2014/01/25/opinion/sunday/
how-long-have-i-got-left.html?smid=url-share

279 Paul Kalanithi, When Breath Becomes Air, New York: Random House,
2016

280 Matthew 26:39-42 KJV

281 Paul Kalanithi, When Breath Becomes Air, New York: Random House,
2016.

282 Y. Dor-Ziderman, "Prediction-based neural mechanisms for shielding
the self from existential threat," Neuroimage,22 (November 15, 2019, https://
doi.org/10.1016/j.neuroimage.2019.116080

283 Ian Sample, "Doubting death: how our brains shield us from mortal
truth," The Guardian, October 19,2019, https://www.theguardian.com/
science/2019/oct/19/doubting-death-how-our-brains-shield-us-from-mortal-
truth

284 John Horgan, "s Scientific Materialism "Almost Certainly False"?" Scientific American, January 30, 2013, https://blogs.scientificamerican.com/
cross-check/is-scientific-materialism-almost-certainly-false/

285 James Pethokoukis, "Nobel Laureate Daniel Kahneman on AI: 'It's Very
Difficult to Imagine That with Sufficient Data There Will Remain Things
That Only Humans Can Do'," January 18, 2011, https://www.aei.org/
economics/nobel-laureate-daniel-kahneman-on-a-i-its-very-difficult-to-
imagine-that-with-sufficient-data-there-will-remain-things-that-only-hu-

mans-can-do/

286 Bernardo Kastrup, Why Materialism Is Baloney: How true skeptics know there is no death and fathom answers to life, the universe, and everything, Winchester UK:Iff Books, 2014.

287 Philip Goff, "Science as we know it can't explain consciousness but a revolution is coming," The Conversation, November 1, 2019, https://theconversation.com/science-as-we-know-it-cant-explain-consciousness-but-a-revolution-is-coming-126143

288 Bernardo Kastrup, "Consciousness Goes Deeper Than You Think," Scientific American, September 19, 2017, https://blogs.scientificamerican.com/observations/consciousness-goes-deeper-than-you-think/

289 Josh Weisberg, "The Hard Problem of Consciousness," Internet Encyclopedia of Philosophy, https://iep.utm.edu/hard-problem-of-concious-ness/

290 Padmasambhava, The Tibetan Book of the Dead, Translated by Gyurme Dorje, New York: Penguin Classics, 2007.

291 Oakridge Boys, "You Don't Have to Go Home (But You Can't Stay Here)." Lyrics, Accessed January, 1, 2010, https://www.lyrics.com/lyric/35894540/The+Oak+Ridge+Boys/You+Don%27t+Have+to+Go+Home+%28But+You+Can%27t+Stay+Here%29

292 Atul Gawande, Being Mortal, New York: Metropolitan Books, 2014

293 Michael Claeys, "Gawande discusses problems of 'medicalized' mortality in the U.S.," Stanford Medicine, March 5, 2015, https://med.stanford.edu/news/all-news/2015/03/gawande-discusses-problems-of-medi-calized-mortality-in-the-us

294 IBID

295 Sam Shead, "Silicon Valley's quest to live forever could benefit humanity as a whole — here's why,"CNBC, September 21, 2021, https://www.cnbc.com/2021/09/21/silicon-valleys-quest-to-live-forever-could-bene-fit-the-rest-of-us.html

296 Mark Piesing, "Silicon Valley's Suicide Pill for Mankind," Unherd, August 20, 2018, https://unherd.com/2018/08/silicon-valleys-suicide-pill-mankind/

297 Anna Gorman, "Diabetic Amputations A 'Shameful Metric' Of Inadequate Care," Kaiser Health News," May 1, 2019, https://khn.org/news/diabetic-amputations-a-shameful-metric-of-inadequate-care/

298 Sean McDonnell, "Where Are the Workers? Project launches website with new data and insights for NE Ohio," July 1, 2022, https://www.

cleveland.com/business/2022/07/where-are-the-workers-project-launches-website-with-new-data-and-insights-for-northeast-ohio.html

299 James Surowiecki, "Always Expect the Unexpected," Wired, April 1, 2007, https://www.wired.com/2007/04/always-expect-the-unexpected/

300 Lao Tzu, Tao Te Ching, Translated by Stephen Mitchell, New York: Harper Collins, 1988.

301 Alexia Fernández Campbell, "Do Parts of the Rust Belt 'Need to Die Off'?" July 20, 2016, https://www.theatlantic.com/business/archive/2016/07/rust-belt-survival/492155/

302 IBID

303 Richey Piiparinen, "Smart Decline is Dumb-Why Cities Can't Manage Decline," Atlantic City Lab, March 5, 2017, https://www.bloomberg.com/news/articles/2017-03-05/why-cities-can-t-manage-decline

304 "Office of the Mayor, Mayor Bibb's Rescue & Transformation Plan, Inclusive Economic Recovery, accessed December, 26,2022, https://mayor.clevelandohio.gov/initiatives/mayor-bibbs-rescue-transformation-plan

305 Franz Kafka, Metamorphosis, Leipzig: Kurt Wolff, 1915

306 Gunmar Branson, "Tightening the Belts: Rethinking Sun vs. Rust," Summit Journal, March 25, 2021,https://www.afire.org/summit/sunvsrust/#notes

307 Hannah Richie et al., "Five key findings from the 2022 UN Population Prospects," Our World in Data, July 11, 2022, https://ourworldindata.org/world-population-update-2022

308 Max Roser and Lucas Rodés-Guirao, "Future of Population Growth," Our World in Data, November, 2019, https://ourworldindata.org/future-population-growth#citation

309 "U.CA. Census Bureau, Our Services and Programs, Population and Housing Estimates, 2020-2021, Author's Calculations, https://www.census.gov/programs-surveys/popest.html

310 Reid Wilson, "3 out of 4 US counties had more deaths than births in past year," The Hill, March, 25, 2022, https://thehill.com/homenews/state-watch/599584-3-out-of-4-us-counties-had-more-deaths-than-births-in-past-year/

311 Aldous Huxley, Brave New World, London: Chatto & Windus, 1932.

312 A J. Gyourko, C. Mayer, C. and T. Sinai, T. (2013). "Superstar Cities," American Economic Journal: Economic Policy, 5, no.4(November 3013): 167-199, (http://dx.doi.org/10.1257/pol.5.4.167

313 Samuel Arbesman, "Warning: your reality is out of date," The Boston Globe, February 28, 2010, http://archive.boston.com/bostonglobe/ideas/articles/2010/02/28/warning_your_reality_is_out_of_date/

314 U.S. Bureau of Economic Analysis, "MARPI Real personal income by MSA (accessed Sunday, January 8, 2023)

315 James Pethokoukis, "Nobel Laureate Daniel Kahneman on AI: 'It's Very Difficult to Imagine That with Sufficient Data There Will Remain Things That Only Humans Can Do'," January 18,2011, https://www.aei.org/economics/nobel-laureate-daniel-kahneman-on-a-i-its-very-difficult-to-imagine-that-with-sufficient-data-there-will-remain-things-that-only-humans-can-do/

316 Michael Lewis, The Undoing Project, New York:W.W. Norton & Company,2016

317 Jason Hackworth, "Demolition as urban policy in the American Rust Belt, "Environment and Planning A, 48, issue 11 (November 2016):2201-22222, https://doi.org/10.1177/0308518X16654914

318 Steve Hendrick, "Life, Death, and Demolition, The Washington Post, March, 22, 2017, https://www.washingtonpost.com/graphics/local/baltimore-life-death-and-demolition/

319 Guy De Meo, Subjectivity, Sociality and Spatiality: The Body as the Geographical Unthought," Annales de géographie, 675. Issue 5 (September 2010): 466-491, https://www.cairn-int.info/journal-annales-de-geographie-2010-5-page-466.htm

320 Freeview, "Big South Side Area is Getting Her Face Lifted," Chicago Tribune, 1951, https://www.newspapers.com/clip/33079938/south-side-land-clearance-1951/

321"Cambridge Dictionary, dictionary, English, blight, accessed December 26,2022, https://dictionary.cambridge.org/us/dictionary/english/blight

322 "National Health Services, Mental Health, skin picking disorders, last reviewed March, 2021, https://www.nhs.uk/mental-health/conditions/skin-picking-disorder/

323 "History on the Net, Authentic History, 1898-1913,Progressivism, Riis, accessed December 26,2022, https://www.historyonthenet.com/authentichistory/1898-1913/2-progressivism/2-riis/index.html

324 Jimmy Fyfe, "Exposing the poverty in New York's underbelly," Copenhagen Post Online, March 7, 2016, https://cphpost.dk/?p=5311

325 "University of Virginia, American Studies, City Beautiful Movement," accessed December 26,2022, http://xroads.virginia.edu/~CAP/CITYBEAUTI-

FUL/city.html

326 Paul Boyer, "The Ideology of the Civic Arts Movement in America 1890-1920, The Houston Review, 2, no.1 (Winter 1980):5-19, https://houstonhistorymagazine.org/wp-content/uploads/2014/02/The-Ideology-of-the-Civic-Arts-Movement-in-America-1890-1920

327 Modern Civic Art or The City Made Beautiful, New York and London: G.P. Putnam's and Sons, 1904.

328 "The Library of Consciousness, The Tao of Philosophy, Program 5 Myth of Myself, accessed January, 10, 2023, https://www.organism.earth/library/document/tao-of-philosophy-5

329 Urban Conflagration and the Making of the Modern World. Madison: University of Wisconsin Press, 2012, https://muse.jhu.edu/chapter/654109

330 Daniel Kerr, "Who Burned Cleveland, Ohio?" The Forgotten Fires of the 1970s' in "Flammable Cities, Urban Conflagration and the Making of the Modern World. Madison: University of Wisconsin Press, 2012. https://muse.jhu.edu/chapter/654109

331 U.S. Census Bureau, Decennial Census, 1900 to 1980, Author's Calculations.

332 Alaa Gharbawi, Revolution of the Internet," https://sites.cs.ucsb.edu/~almeroth/classes/F04.176A/homework1_good_papers/Alaa-Gharbawi.html-

333 "Wikipedia, Article, Afterlife, last edited December 25,2022, https://en.wikipedia.org/wiki/Afterlife

334 "The Church of Jesus Christ of Latter Day Saints, life has purpose, what happens after we die?" accessed December 26,2022, https://www.churchofjesuschrist.org/comeuntochrist/believe/life-has-purpose/what-happens-after-we-die

335"The Cleveland Clinic, Health Library, Articles, What happens when you die? What happens to your physical body when you die?" last reviewed, May 27,2022, https://my.clevelandclinic.org/health/articles/23144-what-happens-when-you-die

336 Richard Vitzhum, Materialism: An Affirmative History and Definition, Buffalo, NY: Prometheus Books, 1995

337 Bernardo Kastrup, Why Materialism is Baloney, Winchester UK: Iff Books, 2013.

338 Ernst J. Öpik, "About Dogma in Science and Other Recollections as an Astronomer," Annual Review of Astronomy and Astrophysics,15 (September 1977):1-18, https://doi.org/10.1146/annurev.aa.15.090177.000245

339 Avi Loeb, "When Scientific Orthodoxy Resembles Religious Dogma," Scientific American, May 17, 2021, https://www.scientificamerican.com/article/when-scientific-orthodoxy-resembles-religious-dogma/

340 IBID

341 IBID
342 "David Papke, "Karl Marx on Religion, "Marquette University Faculty Blog, January 20, 2015, https://law.marquette.edu/facultyblog/2015/01/karl-marx-on-religion/comment-page-1/

343 Job 10:11 NLT

344 Benjamin Zeller, "Steve Jobs and the Cult of Apple," University of Chicago Divinity School, October 20,2011, https://divinity.uchicago.edu/sightings/articles/steve-jobs-and-cult-apple-benjamin-e-zeller

345 Soren Kierkegaard, The Present Age and of the Difference Between a Genius and an Apostle, New York: Harper & Row, 1962.

346 "University of Virginia School of Medicine, Division of Perceptual Studies, Near Death Experience, accessed January, 27, 2023, https://med.virginia.edu/perceptual-studies/our-research/near-death-experiences-ndes/

347 "National Institutes of Health, publications, dictionary, second line of therapy, accessed December, 27,2022, https://www.cancer.gov/publications/dictionaries/cancer-terms/def/second-line-therapy

348 OECD (2023), Health spending (indicator). doi: 10.1787/8643de7e-en (Accessed on 11 January 2023)

349 "National Institutes of Health, publications, dictionary, progression-free survival, accessed December, 27,2022,https://www.cancer.gov/publications/dictionaries/cancer-terms/def/progression-free-survival

350 Ben Williams, Surviving 'Terminal Cancer: Clinical Trials, Drug Cocktails, and Other Treatments Your Oncologist Won't Tell You about. United Kingdom: Fairview Press, 2002.

351 Richard Smith, "Dying of Cancer is the Best Death,"thebmjopinion, December 31, 2014, https://blogs.bmj.com/bmj/2014/12/31/richard-smith-dying-of-cancer-is-the-best-death/

352 Lorna Collier, "Growth after trauma," Monitor on Psychology,47, no.10 (November 2016):48, https://www.apa.org/monitor/2016/11/growth-

353 Silver Lining's Playbook, David Russell (The Weinstein Company,2012) 1 hour, 22 minutes. https://www.imdb.com/title/tt1045658/

354 "Journal Psyche" Jung and His Individuation Process," accessed

December 27, 2022, http://journalpsyche.org/jung-and-his-individuation-process/

355 "Medical News Today, articles. displacement," https://www.medical-newstoday.com/articles/displacement-psychology, last reviewed May18,2022

356 Alan Watts, Wisdom of Insecurity, United Kingdom: Rider, 1989.

357 Arthur Koestler, JR Smythies, eds. Beyond Reductionism: New Perspectives on the Life Sciences. Boston: Houghton Mifflin Co; 1971.

358 Kurt Strange, "A Science of Connectedness," Annals of Family Medicine7, no. 5 (September 2009):387-395, DOI: https://doi.org/10.1370/afm.990

359 Laura Gottlieb, "The Social Determinants of Health: It's Time to Consider the Causes of the Causes," Public Health Reports, 129 suppl. 2 (Jan.-Feb. 2014):19-31, https://doi.org/10.1177/00333549141291S

360 Simon Rogers, "Bobby Kennedy on GDP: 'measures everything except that which is worthwhile'", The Guardian, May, 24, 2021, https://www.theguardian.com/news/datablog/2012/may/24/robert-kennedy-gdp

361 "Census Reporter, Census Tract 1171.01, Cuyahoga, OH, accessed January, 5, 2023, https://censusreporter.org/profiles/14000US39035117101-census-tract-117101-cuyahoga-oh/

362 "OECD, Glossary of Statistical Terms, Knowledge-Based Economy," created on September 9, 2005, https://stats.oecd.org/glossary/detail.asp?ID=6864

363 Amanda Aronczyk, "Blood money," National Public Radio Planet Money, May 14, 2021, https://www.npr.org/transcripts/996921658

364 IBID

365 IBID

366 S.Kukushkin, "Four-Sector Model Economy," Vestnik of the Plekhanov Russian University of Economics,1. No.1 (February 2020):25-31,bhttps://doi.org/10.21686/2413-2829-2020-1-25-31

367 Dazhong Cheng, "The development of the service industry in the modern economy: mechanisms and implications for China," China Finance and Economic Review, 1, 3 (December 2013), https://doi.org/10.1186/2196-5633-1-3

368 Kevin Hu and Feng Fu, "Evolutionary Dynamics of Gig Economy Labor Strategies under Technology, Policy and Market Influence," Game, 2, no. 2 (June 2021): 49, https://doi.org/10.3390/g12020049

369 Ben Zipperer et al., "National survey of gig workers paints a picture of poor working conditions, low pay," Report, Economic Policy institute, June 1, 2022, https://www.epi.org/publication/gig-worker-survey/

370 David Autor, "Work of the past, work of the future, "Center for Economic Policy Research, March 19,2019, https://cepr.org/voxeu/columns/work-past-work-future

371 Peter Drucker, The Age of Discontinuity: Guidelines to Our Changing Society. United States: Transaction Publishers, 2011.

372 Peter Drucker, Post-Capitalist Society. New York: Harper Business, 1993.

373 Delloitte Access Economics, "Premium skills: The wage premium associated with human skills," 2019, https://www2.deloitte.com/content/dam/Deloitte/au/Documents/Economics/deloitte-au-economics-premium-skills-deakinco-060120.pdf

374 Thomas Edsall, "Why Do We Pay So Many People So Little Money?" New York Times, June 24, 2020, https://www.nytimes.com/2020/06/24/opinion/wages-coronavirus.html?action=click&module=Opinion&pgtype=Homepage

375 Dhruv Khullar," The Essential Workers Filling New York's Coronavirus Wards," The New Yorker, May 1, 2020, https://www.newyorker.com/science/medical-dispatch/the-essential-workers-filling-new-yorks-coronavirus-wards

376 "Columbia Surgery, COVID-19 Update from Dr. Smith: 4/8/20," accessed December, 28,2022, https://columbiasurgery.org/news/covid-19-update-dr-smith-4820

377 Tal Modai-Snir and Panina Plaut, "The analysis of residential sorting trends: Measuring disparities in socio-spatial mobility, "Urban Studiesc,56, issue 2 (2019):288-300, https://doi.org/10.1177/0042098018798759

378 Thomas P.M. Barnett, The Pentagons New Map, New York: Random House, 2004.

379 Thomas P.M. Barnett, "Why the Pentagon Changes Its Maps,"Esquire, September 10, 2016, https://www.esquire.com/news-politics/a1546/thomas-barnett-iraq-war-primer/

380 "Live Science, References, Epigenetics," accessed December 18, 2022, https://www.livescience.com/37703-epigenetics.html

381 Zaneta Thayer and Chris Kuzawa, "Biological memories of past environments: epigenetic pathways to health disparities," Epigenetics,6,7,(July, 2011):793-803, https://doi.org/10.4161/epi.6.7.16222

382 IBID

383 OECD (2023), Life expectancy at birth (indicator). doi: 10.1787/27e0fc9d-en (Accessed on 11 January 2023)

384 IBID

385 OECD (2023), Health spending (indicator). doi: 10.1787/8643de7e-en (Accessed on 11 January 2023)

386 "The progress trap, escaping the progress trap-the book," accessed December 18, 2022, https://progresstrap.org/content/escaping-progress-trap-book

387 Jake Wright "Towards a response to epistemic nihilism." In Alison MacKenzie, Jennifer Rose & Ibrar Bhatt (eds.), The Epistemology of Deceit in a Postdigital Era: Dupery by Design. Springer Nature. pp. 39-59. 2021 ttps://doi.org/10.1007/s42438-021-00270-4

388 Michel Foucault, The Eoucault Reader, New York: Knopf Doubleday Publishing Group, 1984.

389 Richey Piiparinen, Richey; Joshua Valdez, Valdis Krebs, and Jim Russell, "Disrupting Innovation" (2022). All Maxine Goodman Levin School of Urban Affairs Publications. 0123 1773, (June 6, 2022), https://engagedscholarship.csuohio.edu/urban_facpub/1771/

390 Amanda Murray, "Invention Hot Spot: Silicon Valley and the Beginnings of the Computer Revolution in the 1970s," Nielsen Center for the Study of Innovation, June 1 2010, https://invention.si.edu/invention-hot-spot-silicon-valley-and-beginnings-computer-revolution-1970s

391 IBID

392 "Intel, Newsroom," "Intel Breaks Ground in the Silicon Heartland," published September, 9, 2022, https://www.intel.com/content/www/us/en/newsroom/news/intel-breaks-ground-in-the-silicon-heartland.html#gs.m5e91v

393 Richey Piiparinen, Richey; Joshua Valdez, Valdis Krebs, and Jim Russell, "Disrupting Innovation" (2022). All Maxine Goodman Levin School of Urban Affairs Publications. 0123 1773, (June 6, 2022), https://engagedscholarship.csuohio.edu/urban_facpub/1771/

394 IBID

395 Steve Lohr, "Economists Pin More Blame on Tech for Rising Inequality," The New York Times, January 11,2022, https://www.nytimes.com/2022/01/11/technology/income-inequality-technology.html?smid=url-share

396 Kelemwork Cook and DuWain Pinder, "The future of work in Black America," McKinsey Global Institute Analysis, October 2019, https://www.mckinsey.com/~/media/McKinsey/Featured%20Insights/Future%20of%20Organizations/The%20future%20of%20work%20in%20black%20America/The-future-of-work-in-black-America-vF.pdf

397 Kara Swisher, "Elon Musk Is the Id of Tech," The New York Times, August, 16, 2008, https://www.nytimes.com/2018/08/16/opinion/elon-musk-crazy-tesla.html

398 Kathleen O'Toole, Enrico Moretti: The Geography of Jobs," Insights by Stanford Business, https://www.gsb.stanford.edu/insights/enrico-moretti-geography-jobs

399 Nathan Robinson, "Why is San Francisco Covered in Feces?" The Guardian,"August 18, 2018, https://www.theguardian.com/commentis-free/2018/aug/18/san-francisco-poop-problem-inequality-homelessness

400 IBID

401 IBID

403 Sean Miller, "Snapcrap — Why I built an app to report poop on the streets of San Francisco," Medium, January 5, 2019, https://medium.com/@miller.stowe/snapcrap-why-i-built-an-app-to-report-poop-on-the-streets-of-san-francisco-aac12382a7ce

404 Richey Piiparinen, Richey; Joshua Valdez, Valdis Krebs, and Jim Russell, "Disrupting Innovation" (2022). All Maxine Goodman Levin School of Urban Affairs Publications. 0123 1773, (June 6, 2022), https://engagedschol-arship.csuohio.edu/urban_facpub/1771/

405 "NIH National Library of Medicine, Medline Plus, Medical Encyclope-dia, Skull Anatomy, last reviewed August, 18,2020, https://medlineplus.gov/ency/imagepages/8915.htm

406 Amr Abdulazim et al, "Postcraniotomy function of the temporal muscle in skull base surgery: technical note based on a preliminary study," Scientific World Journal, 2012 (March 12, 2022): 5 pages, https://doi.org/10.1100/2012/427081

407 William Stranger, "R. D. Laing: Of Scientism, Spirit, Madness, and the Healing Genius of Relationship," Dharma Café, 2016, http://www.dharmacafe,com/

408 life-cycles/R.-D.-Laing-Of-Scientism-Spirit-Madness-and-the-Healing-Genius-of-Relat/ "Psychology Dictionary, Rebound Effect, created April 28, 2013, accessed December 12, 2022, https://psychologydictionary.org/rebound-effect/

409 Ann Ulanov, "Transference, the transcendent function, and transcen-

dence," Analytical Psychology, 42, 1 (June 28, 2008):119-138, https://doi.org/10.1111/j.1465-5922.1997.00119.x

410 Marcus Chown, "Our Universe may have a fifth dimension that would change everything we know about physics," BBC Science Focus, November 4, 2021, https://www.sciencefocus.com/space/fifth-dimension/

411 IBID

412 Oliver Burkeman, "How to Changer Your Mind:the New Science of Michael Pollan-review," May 22,2018, https://www.theguardian.com/books/2018/may/22/how-to-change-mind-new-science-psychedelics-michael-pollan-review

413 Nicholas Maxwell, "From Knowledge to Wisdom: The Need for an Academic Revolution," (Published in R. Barnett and N. Maxwell, eds., Wisdom in the University, London: Routledge 2008.

414 IBID

415 Tristan Harris, "Our Brains Are No Match for Our Technology," The New York Times, December 5, 2019, https://www.nytimes.com/2019/12/05/opinion/digital-technology-brain.html?smid=url-share

416 Thomas Leatham, "The dark side of John Lennon song 'Working Class Hero'," Far Out Magazine, October 16,2022, https://faroutmagazine.co.uk/dark-side-john-lennon-working-class-hero/

417 Lewis Mumford, The City in History, its Transformations and its Propsects The Bahamas: Harcourt, Brace & World, 1989.

418 IBID

419 "Meeting of the Minds, Society, Understanding the Soul of a City," created February 2016, 2018, accessed December 8, 2022, https://meetingoftheminds.org/understanding-soul-city-25207

419 IBID

420 Andrea Anesi, "Towards a scientific interpretation of the terroir concept: plasticity of the grape berry metabolome," BMC Plant Biology, 191, (August 2015), https://doi.org/10.1186/s12870-015-0584-4

421 "Islay Whiskey Academy, Terroir: of the land," accessed January, 10, 2023, https://islaywhiskyacademy.scot/terroir-in-gaelic-is-anam-an-fhear-rain-soul-of-the-land/

422 Viktor Frankl, Man's Search for Meaning: An Introduction to Logotherapy Boston: Beacon Press, 1962